ESTABLISHING THE DIVINE ENTITY OF ONE LOVE

AF438372

Kwami Kartara
Establishing the Divine Entity of One Love

All rights reserved
Copyright © 2025 by Kwami Kartara

No part of this publication may be reproduced, distributed, or transmitted in any form or by any means, including photocopying, recording, or other electronic or mechanical methods, without the prior written permission of the publisher, except in the case of brief quotations embodied in critical reviews and certain other noncommercial uses permitted by copyright law.

Published by Spines
ISBN: 979-8-89691-721-2

ESTABLISHING THE DIVINE ENTITY OF ONE LOVE

OUR CREATOR'S APOCALYPTIC MESSAGE

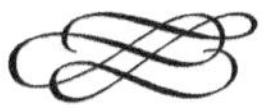

KWAMI KARTARA

CONTENTS

INTRODUCTION

This book will give an account of an upcoming Universal Trial proceeding called the Judgment of True Love. The Defendant is a Spiritual Entity, and this is the Defense's opening statement. In these Universal Trial proceedings, Humankind will become Jurors who will individually establish their own Disposition to settle the Spiritual Conflict between Good and Evil.

This book will present Humankind with the testimony of a Spiritual Perspective that declares all of the world's religions are "tainted." This book will outline a viewpoint that depicts the purpose of Evil and explains our Creator's Plan to restore the Earth and establish a positive living for Humankind to live "with" the Person of God within the United Kingdoms of Heaven and Earth.

This book will provide Humankind with a unique and actual side to the story of our creation as Human beings, which institutes the purpose of our Existence in relation to the ever-developing creation of the Universe.

Testimony will begin with an explanatory summary of the Origins of our Universe and Humankind's creation and will continue with the accounts of the initiation of the Spiritual Conflict between Good and Evil and the instituting of the Due Process to settle the Spiritual Conflict between Good and Evil.

Testimony will introduce evidence that will challenge Humankind to either accept or reject the viewpoint of the established Realities of Truth, from which each person will Spiritually solidify their own Stance with God.

The book will end with an analysis of the Reckoning Disposition of our Creator's Omnipotent Court of Universal Law.

This book is thought-provoking but is not intended to convince the reader of its authenticity, because only God will validate what is Absolute Truth.

However, the Reader's objective will be to solidify one's own Stance from which to establish their Disposition within the Spiritual Conflict between Good and Evil.

Upon being provided with "all sides of the story" (which includes your understanding of a Religious perspective), it is asked that, as the juror, you read this book from the position of evaluating the factual possibilities that will give meaning to one's own Spiritual Identity, as you determine if the Spiritual Entity that gave this account is Good or Evil.

ARTICLE I
THE PRELIMINARY INSTRUCTIONS TO OUR CREATOR'S OMNIPOTENT COURT OF UNIVERSAL LAW

COURT ORDER OF PROCEEDING

DOCUMENT ONE: THE DEFINITIVE INSTRUCTIONS

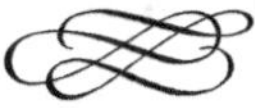

Verse 1

Now, for Humankind's comprehension of the related subject matters, the Definitive Instructions to our Creator's Omnipotent Court of Universal Law – Court Order of Proceeding are as such:

• The Judicial Proceedings for the Confrontation of Truth are our Creator's Omnipotent Court of Universal Law adjudicating the process of vindicating the Love of our Creator as our Heavenly Father's Crowned King of Heaven, and

• The Love of our Creator is the Messiah of Life, in whom is the reincarnated Person of God, "anointed" by our Heavenly Father to be the Crowned King of Heaven – whose duties as the Messiah of Life are to lead Humankind in the Universal

Resurrection to a Positive Existence upon the occurrence of the Apocalypse, and

• The Apocalypse is the Universal Phenomenon of the manifestation of our Heavenly Father divinely revealing to the People of the Earth who actually is the Messiah of Life; and it is the occurrence of the Apocalypse that initiates the Judicial Proceedings for the Confrontation of Truth.

Verse 2

And it is the legal process of the Judicial Proceedings for the Confrontation of Truth that allows the Love of our Creator to Claim his Right to sit upon our Creator's Throne as our Heavenly Father's Crowned King of Heaven; and upon becoming vindicated as our Heavenly Father's Crowned King of Heaven, the Love of our Creator will ascend onto our Creator's Throne – subsequently beginning the Universal Trial proceedings for the Judgment of True Love.

Verse 3

And by definition:

• The Universal Trial proceedings for the Judgment of True Love are our Creator's Omnipotent Court of Universal Law judicial process of evaluating Humankind's Universal Desire to Need to Live "with" the Love of our Creator as our Heavenly Father's Crowned King of Heaven, through an undertaking course that will determine who all are Worthy of living within our Creator's Universal Existence of One Love, and

• Our Creator's Universal Existence of One Love is the everlasting Union of Heaven and Earth, in which our Creator's Spiritual Existence will forever exist within the embodiment of Humankind's creation for Humankind's Universal Existence of an Everlasting Life, living within the Realities of a Positive Existence – upon Humankind being created in the Image and after the Likeness of God, because

• Creating Humankind in the Image and after the Likeness of God is our Creator's process of developing the Perfection of Humankind's creation, from which Humankind must overcome the Evil that exists within the nature of their creation – whereby they may be made capable of sustaining the Energies of a Positive Existence.

Verse 4

And a person who becomes created in the Image and after the Likeness of God will be proven as Worthy of living within our Creator's Universal Existence of One Love.

Verse 5

But it is the legal action taken by our Creator's Omnipotent Court of Universal Law to allow Humankind to experience the Realities of a Negative Existence, which instituted the undertaking course that came to be known as the Spiritual Conflict between Good and Evil.

Verse 6

And by definition, the Spiritual Conflict between Good and Evil is the power clash of a Universal Will to establish the understandings that distinguish a Positive Existence from a Negative Existence.

Verse 7

And from experiencing the Realities of a Negative Existence, it is these Judicial Proceedings for the Confrontation of Truth and the legal action taken to settle the Spiritual Conflict between Good and Evil that start the process of Humankind's Universal Resurrection to the Realities of a Positive Existence.

Verse 8

As it is the understandings ascertained within these Judicial Proceedings for the Confrontation of Truth that will begin vindicating the class-Destinations within our Creator's Universal Existence of One Love – upon each person establishing their own disposition in settling the Spiritual Conflict between Good and Evil.

DOCUMENT TWO: THE ESTABLISHED DISPOSITION IN SETTLING THE SPIRITUAL CONFLICT BETWEEN GOOD AND EVIL

Verse 9

Now, by definition, a person's established Disposition in settling the Spiritual Conflict between Good and Evil is the undertaken Legal Stance to either:

• *produce and develop the habitual tendencies that will Stand With the Spiritual Forces of Good in subduing the Energies of a Negative Existence, or*

• *induce and maintain the habitual tendencies that will Stand With the Forces of Evil in resistance to the Energies that will sustain a Positive Existence.*

Verse 10

And it is in undertaking the course towards becoming proven Worthy of living within our Creator's Universal Existence of One Love that each person must produce and develop the habitual tendencies that will Stand With the Spiritual Forces of Good in subduing the Energies of a Negative Existence – to thereby become created in the Image and after the Likeness of God.

Verse 11

But in order to produce and develop the habitual tendencies that will Stand With the Spiritual Forces of Good in subduing the Energies of a Negative Existence, each person must undertake the course of action to overcome the Evil that exists within the nature of their creation.

Verse 12

Because by undertaking the course of action to overcome the Evil that exists within the nature of their creation, that will be each person's Cooperative Servitude in producing and developing the habitual tendencies that will Stand With the Spiritual Forces of Good in subduing the Energies of a Negative Existence for Humankind's Universal Resurrection to a Positive Existence.

Verse 13

But let it be understood that in order to establish the Disposition that will overcome the Evil that exists within the nature of a person's creation, that person must first choose to take the Legal Stance that will display their Desire to Need to Live with the Love of our Creator as our Heavenly Father's Crowned King of Heaven – because Only the Love of our Creator, upon living within the Realities of a Negative

Existence as the Messiah of Life, has the Disposition and Direction that will lead Humankind in the Universal Resurrection to a Positive Existence.

Verse 14

And it is herein these Judicial Proceedings for the Confrontation of Truth that the Love of our Creator will present Humankind with the Substantiated Evidence of being Worthy of sitting upon our Creator's Throne as our Heavenly Father's Crowned King of Heaven – to hereby give Humankind the Free Will to choose to either:

A. take the Legal Stance that displays their Desire to Need to Live "with" the Love of our Creator as our Heavenly Father's Crowned King of Heaven, or

B. take the Legal Stance that displays their Desire to Need to Live "without" the Love of our Creator as our Heavenly Father's Crowned King of Heaven.

Verse 15

And upon making the choice to take the Legal Stance that displays their Desire to Need to Live "with" the Love of our Creator as our Heavenly Father's Crowned King of Heaven, it is in accord with the Universal Trial proceedings for the Judgment of True Love that Humankind will then begin to produce and develop the habitual tendencies that will overcome the Evil that exists within the nature of their creation – to thereby become proven Worthy of living within our Creator's Universal Existence of One Love.

DOCUMENT THREE: THE CASE SUMMARY OF THE SPIRITUAL CONFLICT BETWEEN GOOD AND EVIL

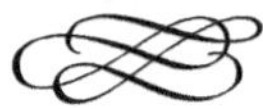

Verse 16

Now, to comprehend the Divine purpose of these legal proceedings, it must be understood that the Spiritual Conflict between Good and Evil began when an Angel known to Humankind as Satan made the Claim that:

Living in accordance with an Unconditional Law of existing would be "More Pleasurable" than living in accordance with our Creator's Universal Laws of Existence.

Verse 17

And with this Claim, Satan accused the Person of God of lying to Humankind and making restrictions that limit the potential of other creations so that no one else could prove to be more Worthy of sitting upon our Creator's Throne as the Crowned King of Heaven.

Verse 18

And in Satan's continuous endeavor to defy the Person of God, Satan trespassed into the Paradise Garden of Heaven and deceived a Woman into having Unmarital Sex with him —thereby producing the Collaborating Evidence intended to prove that Humankind will Not Surely Die from the fruits of violating our Creator's Sacred Rites of Marriage.

Verse 19

And although this act of Infidelity between Satan and the Woman created the First Cause of Action against our Creator's Universal Laws of Existence, it was decided by our Creator's Omnipotent Court of Universal Law that, due to Humankind not having an Objective Understanding of the Relativity of God, before a Ruling can be made to punish Satan for his defiance, the Court must, by Due Process of Universal Law, establish that Satan's Allegations against the Person of God are "False" and prove that Humankind will "Surely Die" from the fruits of violating our Creator's Sacred Rites of Marriage, as proclaimed by the Person of God.

Verse 20

And therefore, a Motion to Remand Satan onto the Kingdoms of the Earth was enacted by our Creator's Omnipotent Court of Universal Law, which gave Satan six (6) thousand years of Dominion upon the Earth's living, to thereby institute the undertaking course that will produce the Trial Evidence needed to prove that living in accordance with an Unconditional Law of existing is "More Pleasurable" than living in accordance with our Creator's Universal Laws of Existence.

Verse 21

And with this Motion to Remand Satan onto the Kingdoms of the Earth, a Universal Decree was issued by our Creator's Omnipotent Court of Universal Law, which closed the Gates of Heaven and ordered everyone who resided within the Kingdom of Heaven (including the Person of God) and everyone who resides within the Kingdoms of the Earth to experience the Realities of a Negative Existence, thereby embarking upon the undertaking course to settle the Spiritual Conflict between Good and Evil.

Verse 22

Wherein, the allotted Time needed for Satan to prove his Claim that living in accordance with an Unconditional Law of existing is "More Pleasurable" than living in accordance with our Creator's Universal Laws of Existence was also incorporated into a Time Period that would give Humankind the opportunity to measure each person's Potential of becoming proven Worthy of sitting upon our Creator's Throne as our Heavenly Father's Crowned King of Heaven.

Verse 23

Because it was ascribed by our Creator's Omnipotent Court of Universal Law that upon living within the Realities of a Negative Existence, it is the inherent Strength and Ability to establish the Disposition and Direction that leads Humankind in the Universal Resurrection to a Positive Existence that will be the Substantiated Evidence proving a Person possesses the Potential needed to be Worthy of sitting upon our Creator's Throne as our Heavenly Father's Crowned King of Heaven.

Verse 24

And at the End-Time of Satan's six (6) thousand years of Dominion upon the Earth's living, it will be at the occurrence of the Apocalypse that our Creator's Omnipotent Court of Universal Law will initiate the Judicial Proceedings for the Confrontation of Truth, thereby resolving the enacted Motion to Suppress Satan's Allegation that God makes restrictions that limit the potential of other creations.

Verse 25

And during these Judicial Proceedings for the Confrontation of Truth, our Heavenly Father will "Challenge" Humankind to stand against the One whom our Heavenly Father is divinely revealing as the Messiah of Life—who will establish the Fundamental Truth that will enable our Creator's Omnipotent Court of Universal Law to execute the Ruling that will cast Satan and his followers into an Eternal Existence of Death.

Verse 26

Because upon giving all of Humankind the opportunity to measure their own Potential of being proven Worthy of sitting upon our Creator's Throne, it will be established during these Judicial Proceedings for the Confrontation of Truth that no one other than the One Person whom our Heavenly Father is divinely revealing as the Messiah of Life has been able to overcome the Powers of Evil—from which to establish the Disposition and Direction that will lead Humankind in the Universal Resurrection to a Positive Existence, thus proving to be the Only One Worthy of sitting upon our Creator's Throne as our Heavenly Father's Crowned King of Heaven.

DOCUMENT FOUR: ESTABLISHING THE VENUE AND JURISDICTIONS FOR THE CONFRONTATION OF TRUTH

Verse 27

Now, to proceed forward with the Judicial proceedings for the Confrontation of Truth, we must first put our present occurrences into perspective, thereby comprehending the Universal Reality that establishes the Venue and Jurisdictions for the Confrontation of Truth—because, as human beings of different nationalities, cultural backgrounds, and spiritual beliefs, we all have our own Perspective of Belief, which is each person's own subjective evaluation and point of view of what they believe and perceive to be Reality and Truth.

Verse 28

And whether you are part of a religion, cult, or whether you believe in a spiritual doctrine or not, every person has a Perspective of Belief—because we all have our own perceptions of what we believe to be reality and truth, which are based on our own experiences and the views we were taught. Meaning, we can all be looking at the same divine phenomenon, but depending on the views of our belief, each of us can have a different perspective of what is occurring.

Verse 29

And it is to be understood that within the Realities of our Universal Existence, you have your Perspective of Belief, others have theirs, and then there is the Fundamental Truth of God—which is the perspective substantiated by our Heavenly Father as the basic Truth of our Universal Reality.

Verse 30

And as Human beings living within the Realities of a Negative Existence, surrounded by so much chaos and confusion in our world's living due to the many lies and liars, past and present, who have promoted and profited from the Manipulation of Truth—it must be clarified that although we all have our own Perspectives of Belief, only our Heavenly Father, who is the Creator of our Universal Existence, can substantiate a Perspective of Belief as the Fundamental Truth of God.

Verse 31

And the only Perspective of Belief that our Heavenly Father will substantiate as the Fundamental Truth of God is the one perceived by the one person whom our Heavenly Father has raised to be the Messiah of Life—because, upon living within the Realities of a Negative Existence, it is the Messiah of Life, whose experiences and views were guided by our Heavenly Father, who stands as the vantage point that will measure and give meaning to the basic Truth of our Universal Reality.

Verse 32

And therefore, in relation to establishing the Venue for the Confrontation of Truth—understand that these judicial proceedings are displayed upon a Universal stage, so that all the people of the Earth may witness our Heavenly Father substantiate the Perspective of Belief that is the Fundamental Truth of God.

Verse 33

And in establishing the Venue for the Confrontation of Truth, it is the Apocalypse that designates all the Kingdoms of the Earth as the localities in which a Universal Trial will be held to settle the Spiritual Conflict between Good and Evil— as it is the Apocalypse and the occurrences thereof that form the manner in which our Heavenly Father will divinely reveal to the People of the Earth who truly is the Messiah of Life.

Verse 34

And in relation to establishing the Jurisdictions for the Confrontation of Truth—it is herein, within these judicial proceedings, that the actual Messiah of Life will Claim his right to sit upon our Creator's Throne as our Heavenly Father's Crowned King of Heaven, while giving the People of the Earth the Perspective of Belief that is the Fundamental Truth of God.

Verse 35

And in establishing the Jurisdictions for the Confrontation of Truth, it is the testimony of the Messiah of Life that addresses and acknowledges our Creator's Omnipotent Court of Universal Law as the presiding Authority that will evaluate Humankind's Desire and Need to Live with the Love of our Creator—as our Heavenly Father's Crowned King of Heaven, for the Judgment of True Love.

Verse 36

And upon revealing who the Messiah of Life is, our Heavenly Father will expose the lies and liars, past and present, who promoted and profited from the Manipulation of the Truth —as these judicial proceedings will be conducted in a manner that will challenge anyone to stand against who our Heavenly Father is divinely revealing as the Messiah of Life; which is why these Judicial proceedings are called the Confrontation of Truth.

Verse 37

And in putting our present occurrences into perspective with these Judicial proceedings for the Confrontation of Truth, it must be clarified that although you may believe in a certain name or person to be the Messiah—if you are not the one whom our Heavenly Father is divinely revealing as the

Messiah of Life, then you are hereby ordered to remain silent.

Verse 38

And if he whom you believe to be the Messiah is the actual Messiah of Life, then it is within these Judicial proceedings for the Confrontation of Truth that he (himself) must speak the Fundamental Truth of God and Claim his own right to sit upon our Creator's Throne as our Heavenly Father's Crowned King of Heaven.

Verse 39

And let it be clarified that Humankind does not have the right or power to choose "who they want to be the Messiah of Life," but it is herein these Judicial proceedings for the Confrontation of Truth that Humankind will be given the Free Will to choose to either accept or reject the one whom our Heavenly Father is divinely revealing as the Messiah of Life.

Verse 40

And let it be understood that whoever "rejects" the one who is divinely revealed as the Messiah of Life or "objects" to the Perspective of Belief that is substantiated by our Heavenly Father as the Fundamental Truth of God—that person(s) will be held in contempt of our Creator's Omnipotent Court of Universal Law, and they will be Stricken by our Creator and consequently cast into an Eternal Existence of Death.

Verse 41

And being that the Messiah of Life is the Love of our Creator, who is the reincarnated Person of God:

To accept the Messiah of Life as our Heavenly Father's Crowned King of Heaven will be taking the legal stance to begin putting forth the efforts to produce and develop the habitual tendencies that will stand with the Spiritual Forces of Good in subduing the Energies of a Negative Existence—whereby establishing the Disposition that will overcome the Evil that exists within the nature of their creation,

-but-

To reject the Messiah of Life as our Heavenly Father's Crowned King of Heaven or object to his Perspective of Belief as the Fundamental Truth of God will be taking the legal stance to continue to induce and maintain the habitual tendencies that will stand with the Forces of Evil in resistance to the Energies of a Positive Existence—whereby establishing the Disposition that knowingly and willingly opposes the Will of God.

Verse 42

And so, in perspective with establishing the Venue and Jurisdictions for the Confrontation of Truth, the bottom line is that, all while living within the Realities of a Negative Existence, Satan has had dominion upon the Earth's living—which means that under Satan's rule, all the religions of the world are tainted, all the governments of the world are corrupted, and all the People of the world are deceived.

Verse 43

And at the end time of Satan's Rule, do not be a fool and Claim something for someone else, because just as there is a Messiah of Life who will lead Humankind in our Universal Resurrection to a positive existence—there is also a Messiah of Death who has misled the people of the Earth to believe that he was the Messiah of Life, in hopes of luring as many people as possible into an Eternal Existence of Death with him.

ARTICLE II
MEASURING OUR PERSPECTIVES OF BELIEF

THE TRIAL EXAMINATION

Verse 1

To Measure our Perspectives of Belief, we will evaluate through Trial examination—our Faith in the existence of our Creator as a Supreme Being—to thereby ascertain the relative positioning between a person's Perspective of Truth and the Fundamental Truth of God; wherein we will learn the basic requirement for being able to live within the United Kingdoms of Heaven and Earth, as well as the qualifications for being able to Stand as the Messiah of Life.

Verse 2

Now, by definition, having Faith in the existence of our Creator as a Supreme Being means having Confidence and Trust that our Creator exists as a Supreme Being who functions within our Universe for the betterment of Humankind's creation.

Verse 3

And in our quest for evidence of the existence of our Creator as a Supreme Being, we look at our Universe producing Life within the scope of its created complexity—and when we see how Life and our Universe are so perfectly designed and arranged to function in an orderly manner (from the solar system within our Universe to the bodily systems within our human creation), it is only instinctive to believe that an all-powerful and highly intelligent Creator has created our Universe to produce Life.

Verse 4

But questions concerning the existence of our Creator as a Supreme Being arise when we, as human beings, look at the Realities of our Universal Existence living together upon the Earth.

Verse 5

And when we look at the Realities of our Universal Existence living together upon the Earth, our realities are negative because we are living in a world filled with so much evil, death, violence, hatred, deception, misery, and ill epidemics—all due to the Cause and Effects of Sin.

Verse 6

And although Life, in its essence, is so very beautiful, the way that we are living together upon the Earth makes living Life ugly and hard. But if a Creator exists as a Supreme Being who can create such a perfectly designed universe to produce Life, then why would this same all-powerful and highly intelligent Creator not design a better way for Humankind to live together upon the Earth?

Verse 7

And so it was the actualities of living within the Realities of a Negative Existence that became the Trial examination that challenges Humankind's Faith in the existence of our Creator as a Supreme Being—whereby to develop and evaluate each person's confidence and trust that our Creator, as a Supreme Being, will function through creation to make a better way for Humankind to live together upon the Earth.

THE EVALUATION

Verse 8

Now, if you did not believe in God and believed that Life just happened to create itself, and you lived with no manners of Respect, no Moral Principles, and no Purpose in contributing to making Life better for all of Humankind, and with no God's conscience, you took advantage of and/or profited from the suffering, abuse, and/or ignorance of the weak, humble, and less fortunate—then you have a Negative Perspective of Belief, because you lived with no Confidence and no Trust that our Creator, as a Supreme Being, will function through creation to make a better way for Humankind to live together upon the Earth; and this Position of Reality is in opposition to the Fundamental Truth of God.

Verse 9

But if you believed in God and believed that there is a Divine Purpose to why our Creator has allowed Humankind to live within the Realities of a Negative Existence, and in giving meaning to this Divine Purpose, you tried living with moral principles, integrity, and dignity while trying to contribute to the betterment of others—then you have a Positive Perspective of Belief, because you lived with Confidence and Trust that our Creator, as a Supreme Being, will function through creation to one day make a better way for Humankind to live together upon the Earth; and this Position of Reality is in unison with the Fundamental Truth of God.

Verse 10

And whether small or great, if you had Faith in the existence of our Creator as a Supreme Being while living within the Realities of a Negative Existence, then you understood that our challenge of living upon the Earth was not about our Creator's existence as a Supreme Being or His ability to make a better way for Humankind to live—but instead, our challenge of living within the Realities of a Negative Existence was about us, as individuals, being able to live in the designs of living together within our Creator's Universal Existence.

Verse 11

And being able to live in the designs of living together within our Creator's Universal Existence means being individuals capable of functioning in harmony with one another despite our differences in nationality, race, culture, sex, age, or abilities—as our capabilities of functioning in harmony with others while living within the Realities of a Negative Existence become the evaluation that measures each person's Faith in the existence of our Creator as a Supreme Being.

THE MEASUREMENT

Verse 12

Now, in this time when our Creator, as a Supreme Being, will make a better way for Humankind to live together upon the Earth, those who have a Positive Perspective of Belief will qualify as being Able to live within the Designs of living together within the United Kingdoms of Heaven and Earth "with" our Creator as a Supreme Being—as they will be in the position to Change from the Realities of a Negative Existence to the Realities of a Positive Existence.

Verse 13

But let it be understood that how we are living upon the Earth is not the same as how it is lived in Heaven, because in Heaven there is No Violence, No Hatred, No Deception, No Misery, No Ill Epidemics, No Evil, and No Death—and to live together within the United Kingdoms of Heaven and

Earth "with" our Creator as a Supreme Being, there must be a Universal Order for all of Humankind to Change for the Better, from which every Person will be required to be Able to Change from the Realities of a Negative Existence to the Realities of a Positive Existence.

Verse 14

And this Change means to do something different individually and universally because Humankind cannot continue to live the same way together within the same governing System that propels the Realities of a Negative Existence—and to be Able to Change from the Realities of a Negative Existence to the Realities of a Positive Existence, this Universal Order must be coordinated by a System designed and arranged to function in correlation with finding out Who All are Able to live within the Designs of living together within the United Kingdoms of Heaven and Earth, as evaluated by each person's Faith in the existence of our Creator as a Supreme Being.

Verse 15

But in order to design this System that will coordinate a Universal Order to Change from the Realities of a Negative Existence to the Realities of a Positive Existence, there must be a Perspective of Belief that "Exacts the Divine Purpose to the Realities of our Universal Existence"—because, in order for the Powers and Abilities of our Creator's Spiritual Existence to function within our Universe to the effects of Humankind's Universal creation, Humankind's Faith in our

Creator as a Supreme Being must be In Sync with our Creator's Spiritual Existence functioning through creation to make a better way for Humankind to live together upon the Earth; and only through the Faith of a person whose Perspective of Belief fulfills the Divine Purpose to the Realities of our Universal Existence will Humankind obtain the functioning of our Creator's Spiritual Existence within creation.

Verse 16

And by definition, to Exact the Divine Purpose to the Realities of our Universal Existence means to obtain the functioning of our Creator's Spiritual Existence within creation by the authority of that person's Will to manifest the Designs of Humankind living together within the United Kingdoms of Heaven and Earth, in correlation with the Faith that our Creator's Spiritual Existence functions within their creation to process the System for Humankind to live together within our Universal Existence; and only the Messiah of Life, in whose "Belief in himself" is the Authority that can obtain the functioning of our Creator's Spiritual Existence within creation.

Verse 17

Because the created existence of our Creator as a Supreme Being is known as God, and it is the Messiah of Life in whom is the reincarnated Person of God anointed by our Heavenly Father to be the Crowned King of Heaven—who, while living within the Realities of a Negative Existence, is the Only Person whose Perspective of Belief can Exact the Divine Purpose to the Realities of our Universal Existence.

Verse 18

Which means that the Qualifications for being Able to Stand as the Messiah of Life are not only being anointed by our Heavenly Father to be the Crowned King of Heaven, but also having the Confidence and Trust that he possesses the Power and Ability to design a System that will coordinate the Universal Order to Change from the Realities of a Negative Existence to the Realities of a Positive Existence, in correlation with fulfilling the Divine Purpose that will make a better way for Humankind to live together within our Universal Existence.

THE RELATIVE POSITIONING

Verse 19

Now, by definition, the Divine Purpose to the Realities of our Universal Existence is to process the Perfection of Humankind's creation through the Due Process of settling the Spiritual Conflict between Good and Evil.

Verse 20

And to fulfill the Divine Purpose to the Realities of our Universal Existence, Humankind—by settling the Spiritual Conflict between Good and Evil—must be created in the Image and after the Likeness of God, thereby displaying the Capabilities to move within the created functioning of our Universal Existence, "changing" from within the Realities of a Negative Existence to the Realities of a Positive Existence.

Verse 21

And by definition, becoming created in the Image and after the Likeness of God is the developing process of Perfecting Humankind's creation to live in the Designs of living together within the United Kingdoms of Heaven and Earth "with" our Creator as a Supreme Being—in which Humankind must overcome the Evil that exists within the nature of their creation while living within the Realities of a Negative Existence.

Verse 22

And despite any Religious or Spiritual misconceptions, creating Humankind in the Image and after the Likeness of God is not about a created Look, Appearance, or Birthright —it is a Process of Development. And to comprehend this process, Humankind must understand that in the Origins of Creation, our Creator created God from nothing. This means that the developmental process of creating (God)—the Supreme Being of the Universe—progressed from a Negative Existence of being nothing to a Positive Existence of being something.

Verse 23

And from this process of creating the Supreme Being of the Universe:

• *The Image of God became defined as the reflection of Righteous Conduct, and*

• The Likeness of God became defined as the appreciation of a Virtuous Livelihood.

Verse 24

And it is in Perfecting Humankind's creation to live within the Designs of living together within the United Kingdoms of Heaven and Earth "with" our Creator as a Supreme Being that the development of Humankind must also move from a Negative Existence to a Positive Existence.

Verse 25

Because in order for Humankind to live in the Designs of living together within the United Kingdoms of Heaven and Earth "with" our Creator as a Supreme Being, they must experience the Realities of a Negative Existence—to thereby overcome the Evil that exists within the nature of their creation. From this process, Humankind will develop the Strength and Abilities necessary to sustain the Energies of a Positive Existence for an Everlasting Life.

Verse 26

And it is through the developmental process of Perfecting Humankind's creation to live in the Designs of living together within the United Kingdoms of Heaven and Earth "with" our Creator as a Supreme Being that:

(1) Upon our Creator divinely revealing to Humankind who truly is the Messiah of Life, Humankind—in displaying the Strength to subdue the Energies of a Negative Existence—must appreciate the

Virtuous Livelihood of our Creator as a Supreme Being by adhering to the Authority of the Perspective that achieved the functioning of our Creator's Spiritual Existence within creation, which coordinates the Universal Order to transition from the Realities of a Negative Existence to the Realities of a Positive Existence.

(2) While living within the Realities of a Negative Existence, Humankind—in displaying the Abilities to sustain the Energies of a Positive Existence—must reflect the Righteous Conduct required to live within the United Kingdoms of Heaven and Earth "with" our Creator as a Supreme Being by producing and developing the habitual tendencies that overcome the Evil that exists within the nature of their creation.

Verse 27

And in ascertaining the Relative Positioning between a person's perception of Truth and the Fundamental Truth of God, it is the actualities of the Apocalypse that represent the created functioning of our Creator's Spiritual Existence within creation. This functioning will be obtained through the Authority of the Messiah of Life's Faith in the existence of our Creator as a Supreme Being—functioning through him to lead Humankind in the Universal Order to Change from living within the Realities of a Negative Existence to living within the Realities of a Positive Existence. And this Exacts the Divine Purpose to the Realities of our Universal Existence.

ARTICLE III
THE DYNAMICS OF OUR UNIVERSAL CREATION

CHAPTER ONE: THE CREATED EXISTENCE OF OUR CREATOR

Verse 1

The Court Hearing to the Judicial Proceedings for the Confrontation of Truth will begin with a definitive composition to the Dynamics of our Universal Creation, which explains our Creator's Objective for Humankind's existence and cooperation within the Applications of our designed Universal Existence.

Verse 2

And by definition, the Dynamics of our Universal Creation is the composition of the Mental, Spiritual, and Physical mechanics for the operations of Universal Order and Motion within the Physics of the Universe.

Verse 3

And it is the Dynamics of our Universal Creation that will

give meaning to the creative functioning of our Universal Existence, which begins with the Creator's Created Existence – in whom is known to Humankind as God.

Verse 4

Now by definition, God is the creation of our Creator in whose Existence is (3) three-dimensional – (External, Internal, and Foundational), from which each dimension is ruled by separate entities known as the Trinity.

Verse 5

And by definition, the Trinity is the consolidation of our Creator, our Heavenly Father, and the Begotten Son collectively functioning to personify God as the One Supreme Being of the Universe.

And by definition, to personify God as the One Supreme Being of the Universe means to embody the Virtues and Values that represent the personal Qualities and Traits in which display the Attributes that possess the Greatest intelligence, power, and significance within the Universe.

Verse 6

And by understanding the misunderstandings and misconceptions that Humankind may have of the Trinity, let it be clarified that:

(1) The First part of the Trinity is our Creator, and our Creator is the Absolute Entity of the Universe in whom rules the External Dimension of the Universe. And as our Creator,

God is All (All-Knowing, All-Present, All-Powerful) from which the Universe is the Body of our Creator, and we are all creations that are a part of our Creator's Body.

(2) The Second part of the Trinity is our Heavenly Father, and our Heavenly Father is the Divine Entity of our Creator in whom rules the Internal Dimension of the Universe. And as our Heavenly Father, God is our Creator's Spiritual Existence in whom exists and functions as the Creative Energies of our Creator's Desire to Need to Live "within" the Elements of the Universe.

Note: Our Creator, from the substances of the Earth, formed the First Man created, and the Creative Energies of our Creator's Desire to Need to Live "within" the Elements of the Universe gave him Life, and the First Man created became the Incarnated entity of our Creator's Spiritual Existence, and he was the Father of Humankind, in whose Death established our Creator's Spiritual Existence as Humankind's Heavenly Father.

(3) The Third part of the Trinity is the Begotten Son, and the Begotten Son is the Reincarnated entity of our Heavenly Father in whom rules the Foundational Dimension of the Universe. And as the Begotten Son, God is the physical creation and the Love of our Creator in whom lives as a person borne of Humankind to be our Heavenly Father's Crowned King of Heaven.

Verse 7

And from the dimensional functionings of our Creator, our Heavenly Father, and the Begotten Son, the consolidation of those (3) three entities will personify God as the One Supreme Being of the Universe – for the purposes of producing the embodied substance of our Creator's Universal Existence.

Verse 8

Because by personifying God as the One Supreme Being of the Universe, the Trinity of God will induce the execution of the designed Configuration for the embodied substance of our Creator's Universal Existence – whereso to direct the proper Conductivity for the illumination of our Creator's Light; and it is our Creator's Light that defines the Life of our Creator.

CHAPTER TWO: OUR CREATOR'S LIGHT

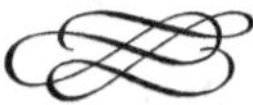

A. Producing the Embodied Substance of Our Creator's Universal Existence

Verse 9

Now by definition, our Creator's Light is the illuminating embodiment of a Universal Desire to Need to Live "with" the Love of our Creator as our Heavenly Father's Crowned King of Heaven – and it is the illumination of our Creator's Light that is the embodied substance of our Creator's Universal Existence in which gives meaning to the Life of our Creator.

Verse 10

And by definition, the Life of our Creator is the awareness of our Creator's Created Existence within the Physics of the Universe – in which distinguishes the Realities of a Positive Existence from the Realities of a Negative Existence.

Verse 11

And the awareness of our Creator's created Existence within the Physics of the Universe is manifested from the "Circuitry" that illuminates our Creator's Light, and by definition – the Circuitry of our Creator's Light is the designed configuration to the procreated Properties of God, Heaven, and Earth being electromagnetically connected to provide an uninterrupted path for Electrical Energy to illuminate our Creator's Light within the Spatial Contents of our Creator's Universal Atmosphere.

Verse 12

And the Circuitry of our Creator's Light is configured to "generate" the Positive Energies needed to "Energize" the Creative Energies of our Creator's Desire to Need to Live within the Elements of the Universe, whereupon "Radiating" the illumination of our Creator's Light from within the Spatial Contents of our Creator's Universal Atmosphere.

Verse 13

And the Circuitry of our Creator's Light is configured as such:

(1) Our Creator created the Elements of the Universe as the Components within the Circuitry of our Creator's Light, (which includes but is not limited to)

A. Heaven, that acts as an Inductor

B. The Earth, that acts as the Generator

C. The Sun, that acts as the Power Source

(2) Our Heavenly Father circuits the Spiritual Beings of Energy as the Electrical Current within the Circuitry of our Creator's Light; and as a Power Source, the Sun is the Harnessed Power to the Creative Energies of our Creator's Desire to Need to Live within the Elements of the Universe – from which all Spiritual Beings of Energy are reproduced.

(3) The Spiritual Beings of Energy are incarnated into Human Beings in whom are created to function as the Conductors of the Electrical Current within the Circuitry of our Creator's Light; and as Humans, our Spiritual Being in which is known as our Soul – derives from our Creator's Spiritual Existence and is genetically reproduced and individualized to be incarnated into the physical form for the purposes of "Generating" the Positive Energies needed to "Energize" the Creative Energies of our Creator's Desire to Need to Live within the Elements of the Universe.

(4) The Begotten Son in whom is the Love of our Creator borne of Humankind to be our Heavenly Father's Crowned King of Heaven will institute the Authoritative Rule for living in accordance with our Creator's Universal Laws of Existence as the Magnetic Force that will induce the execution of the designed Configuration for the embodied substance of our Creator's Universal Existence – which means that the Begotten Son will establish the Direction for

the Earth to operate within the Realities of a Positive Existence.

Verse 14

But in order to "Radiate" the illumination of our Creator's Light from within the Spatial Contents of our Creator's Universal Atmosphere, to thereby produce the embodied substance of our Creator's Universal Existence – the configured Circuitry of our Creator's Light must be executed to "Generate" the Positive Energies needed to "Energize" the Creative Energies of our Creator's Desire to Need to Live within the Elements of the Universe.

Verse 15

And to "Generate" the Positive Energies needed to "Energize" the Creative Energies of our Creator's Desire to Need to Live within the Elements of the Universe, Humankind must Universally Glorify God as the One Supreme Being of the Universe – and by definition, to Glorify God as the One Supreme Being of the Universe means to "Willingly" Worship and Obey the actual Person of God in accord with our Creator's Universal Laws of Existence, whereby to display their Desire to Need to Live "with" the Love of our Creator as our Heavenly Father's Crowned King of Heaven.

Verse 16

And by "Willingly" Worshipping and Obeying the Begotten Son as our Heavenly Father's Crowned King of Heaven,

Humankind will be "Generating" the Positive Energies of a Universal Desire to Need to Live "with" the Love of our Creator as our Heavenly Father's Crowned King of Heaven.

Verse 17

And it is the Positive Energies of a Universal Desire to Need to Live "with" the Love of our Creator as our Heavenly Father's Crowned King of Heaven that are the Positive Energies needed to "Energize" the Creative Energies of our Creator's Desire to Need to Live within the Elements of the Universe – because the Love of our Creator is the physical creation of our Creator living within the Elements of the Universe as the Begotten Son.

B. The Applications of Executing the Designed Configuration for the Embodied Substance of our Creator's Universal Existence.

Verse 18

Now to "Radiate" the illumination of our Creator's Light, the Applications of executing the designed Configuration for the embodied substance of our Creator's Universal Existence must put into action the Cause and Effects required to "Generate" the Positive Energies needed to "Energize" the Creative Energies of our Creator's Desire to Need to Live within the Elements of the Universe.

Verse 19

And by definition, the Applications of Executing the designed Configuration for the embodied substance of our Creator's Universal Existence are the actual applied activities and proceedings coordinated within the operations of Universal Order and Motion designated to perform the created functioning of "Radiating" the illumination of our Creator's Light.

Verse 20

But to execute the designed Configuration for the embodied substance of our Creator's Universal Existence, its Applications must establish the Cause that will "Energize" the Creative Energies of our Creator's Desire to Need to Live within the Elements of the Universe – to thereby create the Effects of "Generating" the Positive Energies needed to "Radiate" the illumination of our Creator's Light.

Verse 21

And so in executing the designed Configuration for the embodied substance of our Creator's Universal Existence, it was constructed by our Creator that:

(1) The Applications of Personifying God as the One Supreme Being of the Universe will establish the Relativity of God, to thereby put into action the Cause that will induce Humankind to "Generate" the Positive Energies of a Universal Desire to Need to Live with the Love of our

Creator as our Heavenly Father's Crowned King of
Heaven, and

(2) The Applications of Glorifying God as the One Supreme
Being of our Universe will measure Humankind's Spiritual
Essence, to thereby create the Effects that will obtain the
Potential Energy required to "Energize" the Creative
Energies of our Creator's Desire to Need to Live within the
Elements of the Universe.

Verse 22

And from the Applications of executing the designed
Configuration for the embodied substance of our Creator's
Universal Existence, the operations of Universal Order and
Motion will initiate the occurrence of the Apocalypse and
open the Gates of Heaven – from which to perform the
creative functioning of "Radiating" the illumination of our
Creator's Light from within the Spatial Contents of our
Creator's Universal Atmosphere.

Verse 23

And it is the creative functioning of "Radiating" the
illumination of our Creator's Light that will Enlighten the
awareness of our Creator's Created Existence within the
Physics of the Universe, thereby giving meaning to the Life
of our Creator and differentiating the Realities of a Positive
Existence from the Realities of a Negative Existence.

Verse 24

And this Enlightenment to the Life of our Creator will

provide Humankind with the Cognizance of a Living God in correlation with the Realities of a Positive Existence, which initiates the Mental Faculties for the operations of Universal Order and Motion within the Physics of the Universe – as the Conscious Architect of our Universal Existence is founded and perceived from the External Dimensions of the Universe, whereupon verifying the Creative and Created Existence of our Creator.

CHAPTER THREE: THE RELATIVITY OF GOD

Verse 25

Now to put into action the Cause that will induce
Humankind to "Generate" the Positive Energies of a
Universal Desire to Need to Live with the Love of our
Creator as our Heavenly Father's Crowned King of Heaven,
a Logic for Glorifying God as the One Supreme Being of the
Universe must be stimulated by the Personification of God
"actually being" the One Supreme Being of the Universe.

Verse 26

Because to be impelled to act and execute within the
designed Configuration for the embodied substance of our
Creator's Universal Existence, Humankind must be inspired
by Valid Reasoning to "Willingly" Worship and Obey the
actual Person of God in accord with our Creator's Universal

Laws of Existence – and it must be Reasoning other than just because God is God.

Verse 27

And this Valid Reasoning to "Willingly" Worship and Obey the actual Person of God must validate the Personification of God as "actually being" the One Supreme Being of the Universe while also providing Humankind with the Cognizance of a Living God in correlation with the Realities of a Positive Existence.

Verse 28

Wherefore, in stimulating a Logic for Glorifying God as the One Supreme Being of the Universe – the Relativity of God must be established by the Trinity of God, from which the Cognizance of a Living God in correlation with the Realities of a Positive Existence will become appreciated by Humankind.

Verse 29

Because by definition, the Relativity of God is Humankind's comprehension of the value and significance that the actual Person of God has in connection with Humankind's existence and well-being.

Verse 30

And to establish the Relativity of God, the collective functioning of our Creator, our Heavenly Father, and the Begotten Son in Personifying God as the One Supreme

Being of the Universe – must show all of Humankind exactly WHY the actual Person of God is Worthy of being Worshipped and Obeyed in accord with our Creator's Universal Laws of Existence as our Heavenly Father's Crowned King of Heaven; and this will be done by Proving,

(1) How others who are not the actual Person of God are Not Worthy of being Glorified as the One Supreme Being of the Universe,

(2) How living without the actual Person of God as our Heavenly Father's Crowned King of Heaven is Not Good,

(3) How Not living in accord with our Creator's Universal Laws of Existence is Not Good, and

(4) How the actual Person of God being our Heavenly Father's Crowned King of Heaven perfects Universal Creation and makes Humankind's living Better and Everlasting.

Verse 31

And this undertaking course to show Humankind exactly Why the actual Person of God is Worthy of being Worshipped and Obeyed in accord with our Creator's Universal Laws of Existence as our Heavenly Father's Crowned King of Heaven became manifested as the Power clash of a Universal Will to distinguish a Positive Existence from a Negative Existence, known as the Spiritual Conflict between Good and Evil – upon which the Personification of God "actually being" the One Supreme Being of the Universe will prove by Due Process, Satan's Claim that living in accordance with an Unconditional Law of existing is not "More Pleasurable" than living in accordance with our Creator's Universal Laws of Existence.

Verse 32

And from the Due Process of settling the Spiritual Conflict between Good and Evil, the Begotten Son, while living within the Realities of a Negative Existence as the Messiah of Life, will institute the Authoritative Rule for living in accordance with our Creator's Universal Laws of Existence – to thereby arrange and direct the operations for Universal Peace, from which Humankind's comprehension of the Value and Significance that the actual Person of God has in connection with Humankind's existence and well-being will become established.

Verse 33

Because in instituting the Authoritative Rule for living in accordance with our Creator's Universal Laws of Existence, the Begotten Son, in whom is the actual Person of God, will lead Humankind in the Direction of living within the Realities of a Positive Existence – whereupon showing Humankind exactly Why he is the Only One Worthy of being Worshipped and Obeyed in accord with our Creator's Universal Laws of Existence as our Heavenly Father's Crowned King of Heaven.

Verse 34

And from establishing the Relativity of God, the Cognizance of a Living God in Correlation with the Realities of a Positive Existence will become appreciated – whereby giving Humankind Valid Reasoning to "Willingly" Worship and Obey the Person of God in accord with our Creator's Universal Laws of Existence, from which stimulating a Logic for Glorifying God as the One Supreme Being of the Universe will put into action the Cause that will induce Humankind to "Generate" the Positive Energies of a Universal Desire to Need to Live with the Love of our Creator as our Heavenly Father's Crowned King of Heaven.

Verse 35

And this stimulated Logic for Glorifying God as the One Supreme Being of the Universe will provide Humankind with the Initiative to Act in relation to the understandings that distinguish a Positive Existence from a Negative Existence, in which establishes the Spiritual Capacities for the operations of Universal Order and Motion within the Physics of the Universe – as the Engineering Will-Power of our Universal Existence is acknowledged and applied from the Internal Dimension of the Universe, whereinto evaluating the Virtues of a Heavenly Lifestyle.

CHAPTER FOUR: HUMANKIND'S SPIRITUAL ESSENCE

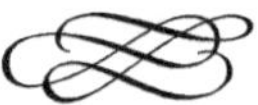

Verse 36

Now to obtain the Potential Energy required to create the Effects that will Energize the Creative Energies of our Creator's Desire to Need to Live within the Elements of the Universe, an Incentive for Glorifying God as the One Supreme Being of the Universe must be promoted within the process of Perfecting Humankind's creation.

Verse 37

Because to produce the constant Execution of "Generating" the Positive Energies of a Universal Desire to Need to Live with the Love of our Creator as our Heavenly Father's Crowned King of Heaven, Humankind must be motivated to Willingly overcome the imperfections of their creation – whereby to be made able to maintain the Energies of a Positive Existence.

Verse 38

And to be made able to maintain the Energies of a Positive Existence, Humankind, upon living within the Realities of a Negative Existence, must by Free Will choose to overcome the Evil that exists within the nature of their creation – to thereby reflect the Initiative to Act in relation to the understandings that distinguish a Positive Existence from a Negative Existence.

Verse 39

Wherefore, in promoting an Incentive for Glorifying God as the Supreme Being of the Universe – Humankind's Spiritual Essence must be measured in correlation with the Due Process of settling the Spiritual Conflict between Good and Evil, from which will the process that perfects their creation "reflect" their Initiative to Act in relation to the understandings that distinguish a Positive Existence from a Negative Existence.

Verse 40

And by definition, Humankind's Spiritual Essence is the Positive or Negative polarized characteristics to the Will-Power of one's Spiritual Being living within the nature of their physical creation.

Verse 41

But to measure Humankind's Spiritual Essence, it must be understood that due to our physical creation being created from the substances of the Earth – the Human Nature of our physical creation is designed to internalize Energy, making Energy flow inwardly into our physical creation; because as physical creations, we need to absorb, inhale, ingest, and consume Energy to maintain our physical living; and this Intake of Energy attributes to the Conductivity for the Negative Polarity within the Circuitry of our Creator's Light as Electrical Current flows from Negative to Positive.

Verse 42

And as our physical creation needs Energy to maintain, our Soul, in which is the charged or (charging) element of our Spiritual Being – is designed to use the Energy internalized into our physical creation to "Generate" more Energy, but as Human Beings in our undeveloped and imperfect state of being, we will Not Only use more Energy than we generate, but we will also generate more Negative Energy than Positive Energy.

Verse 43

And because of that, in order to generate the Positive Energy needed to illuminate our Creator's Light, Humankind's Spiritual Essence must become developed to have control over our Human Nature – which means that as Spiritual Beings living within the physical form, we as Human Beings must by Free Will be made capable of resisting the Evil that derives from within the nature of our creation; Evil such as Lust, Vanity, Greed, Envy, Laziness, Deceit, and Malice.

Verse 44

And so, in the origins of Humankind's creation, it was designed by our Creator that the Essential Characteristics and Will-Power of Humankind's Spirituality would begin with a Neutral Polarity – meaning that in the origins of Humankind's creation, our Souls were neither Positively nor Negatively charged, because along with each Soul's individuality, Free Will was given to allow each Soul the ability to characterize Self and give substance to their own Spiritual Identity through their Incarnated and Reincarnated journeys upon the Earth.

Verse 45

And navigated by our Free Will, it was within the process of perfecting Humankind's creation that our Incarnated and Reincarnated journeys upon the Earth had developed Humankind's Spiritual Essence – because our Incarnated and Reincarnated journeys upon the Earth had matured our Will-Power and materialized the Positive -or- Negative Identity of who we are as a Spiritual Being into the characterisation of who we are as a Person.

Verse 46

And from our Incarnated and Reincarnated journeys upon the Earth, either you became a Good person whose Soul is capable of generating the Positive Energy needed to contribute to the illumination of our Creator's Light -or- you became an Evil person whose Soul is incapable of overcoming the imperfections of their creation.

Verse 47

But to measure Humankind's Spiritual Essence, whereby to determine if a Person is Good or Evil – understand that doing Good things does not instantly make you a Good Person just like doing a Bad thing did not instantly make you an Evil Person, it is the Qualities and Standards that are exemplified by the habitual tendencies of your Attitude, Thoughts, and Actions in which give meaning to the Identity and Will-Power of your Spiritual Being.

Note: Throughout our journeys upon the Earth, Bad People have disguised themselves as Good People and have accused Good People of being Evil while Good People have also Sinned and made Bad mistakes in their Life.

Note: And there have been Lies told throughout Time that have caused many People to believe in False Information and been deceived to commit Negative Acts.

Verse 48

Which is why Humankind's Spiritual Essence is measured in correlation with the Due Process of settling the Spiritual Conflict between Good and Evil, in which processes the Perfection of Humankind's creation through Phases – as it was designed by our Creator that:

(1) The First processing Phase, being the Beginning process of perfecting Humankind's creation, was where our Incarnated journey upon the Earth processed the Goodness

of Humankind's Nature through a Positive living environment that developed the Essential Characteristics of Humankind's Spirituality, and

(2) The Second processing Phase, being the Ending process of perfecting Humankind's creation, was where our Reincarnated journeys upon the Earth processed the Evilness of Humankind's Nature through a Negative living environment that developed the Will-Power of Humankind's Spirituality, and

(3) The Third processing Phase, being the Completing process of perfecting Humankind's creation, is where God's Judgment will measure Humankind's Spiritual Essence in accord with the Criterion promoted by the Authoritative Rule for living in accordance with our Creator's Universal Laws of Existence.

Verse 49

And in correlation with the Due Process of settling the Spiritual Conflict between Good and Evil, the Criterion to measure Humankind's Spiritual Essence will complete the process of perfecting Humankind's creation with an Incentive for Glorifying God as the One Supreme Being of the Universe – in which will configure the Circuitry that generates the Positive Energies needed to Energize the Creative Energies of our Creator's Desire to Need to Live within the Elements of the Universe.

Verse 50

Because the Criterion promoted by the Authoritative Rule for living in accordance with our Creator's Universal Laws of Existence will evaluate Humankind's Desire to Need to Live with the Begotten Son as our Heavenly Father's Crowned King of Heaven, in correlation with Humankind's Will-Power to overcome the Evil that exists within the nature of their creation – from which each and every Person whose Soul is "capable" of generating the Positive Energies of a Universal Desire to Need to Live with the Love of our Creator as our Heavenly Father's Crowned King of Heaven will be given Everlasting Life and Occupation within our Creator's Universal Existence of One Love; while each and every Person whose Soul is "incapable" of overcoming the imperfections of their creation will be cast into an Eternal Existence of Death.

Verse 51

And from the Criterion to measure Humankind's Spiritual Essence, the Initiative to Act in relation to the understandings that distinguish a Positive Existence from a Negative Existence will be reflected – whereby motivating Humankind to "Willingly" overcome the imperfections of their creation, from which will promoting the Incentive for Glorifying God as the One Supreme Being of the Universe obtain the Potential Energy required to create the Effects that will Energize the Creative Energies of our Creator's Desire to Need to Live within the Elements of the Universe.

Verse 52

And this promoted Incentive for Glorifying God as the One Supreme Being of the Universe will provide Humankind with the Ability to exercise Free Will in correlation with perfecting the development of their creation, in which processes the Physical Capabilities for the operations of Universal Order and Motion within the Physics of the Universe – as the Principles that sustain the Growth and Development of our Universal Existence are instituted and ascribed from the Foundational Dimension of the Universe, whereby validating the Values of Humankind's Earthly living.

Verse 53

And so, in conclusion, it is from the Applications of executing the designed Configuration for the embodied substance of our Creator's Universal Existence that the Dynamics of our Universal creation will compose the complete Physics to the Conductivity of our Universal Desire to Need to Live with the Love of our Creator and will be established as the Divine Entity of One Love.

Verse 54

And with the Divine Entity of One Love, the illumination of our Creator's Light (in which is the embodied substance of our Creator's Universal Existence) will solidify within the Physics of the Universe – our Creator's Universal Existence of One Love as the Circuitry that will forever sustain the

Positive Conductivity of a Universal Desire to Need to Live with the Love of our Creator as our Heavenly Father's Crowned King of Heaven, whereby establishing within our Creator's Universal Atmosphere, the Absolute Reality of a Positive Existence.

ARTICLE IV
THE DIVINE ENTITY OF ONE LOVE

PREFACE

The Divine Entity of One Love is the complete Physics to the Conductivity of a Universal Desire to Need to Live with "the Love of our Creator"; in which our Creator's Spiritual Existence will function through Humankind's creation to stabilize the Circuitry that will sustain the illumination of our Creator's Light.

And our Creator's Light is the illuminating embodiment of a Universal Desire to Need to Live with "the Love of our Creator" as the Crowned King of Heaven; in which our Creator's Spiritual Existence will function through the Physics of the Universe to produce the Sustenances that provide Humankind with an Everlasting Life.

But in order to sustain the illumination of our Creator's Light, our Creator must perfect Humankind's creation by "interconnecting":

• the Alpha, which is the Beginning process that conceived the development of Humankind's creation, with

• the Omega, which is the Ending process that perceives the development of Humankind's creation – to thereby formulate

• the Absolute, which is the Completing process that perfects the development of Humankind's creation.

Because in relation to the Circuitry of our Creator's Light:

• the Alpha is the Creative Force that exists within Humankind's creation as the Activated Energies of Love, and in relation to Physics – this Creative Force is the Entity of our Creator's Spiritual Existence as our Heavenly Father, and

• the Omega is the Divine Will-Power that lives within Humankind's creation as "the Love of our Creator," and in relation to Physics – this Divine Will-Power is the Supreme Being of our Creator in whom is the One Begotten Son of our Heavenly Father borne of Humankind to be the Crowned King of Heaven, and

• the Absolute is the Positive Conductivity that interconnects the activated Energies of Love that exist within Humankind's creation with "the Love of our Creator" who lives within Humankind's creation; and in relation to Physics – this Positive Conductivity is the Circuitry that will forever sustain the illumination of our Creator's Light as our Creator's Universal Existence of One Love.

And by definition, our Creator's Universal Existence of One Love is the everlasting Union of Heaven and Earth; in which our Creator's Spiritual Existence will forever exist within the embodiment of Humankind's creation for Humankind's Universal Existence of an Everlasting Life living within the Realities of a Positive Existence.

But it is in formatting the Absolute that an Undertaking Course, which will manifest the Divine Entity of One Love, must determine the class-destinations for living within our Creator's Universal Existence of One Love.

Because in relation to the Illumination of our Creator's Light:

• the Undertaking Course to determine the class-destinations for living within our Creator's Universal Existence of One Love is the Trial Procedure that will create Humankind in the Image and after the Likeness of God; and in relation to Physics – this Trial Procedure is the Legal Proceedings taken to give Humankind the Free Will to display their Desire to Need to Live with "the Love of our Creator" as our Heavenly Father's Crowned King of Heaven and will be known as the Universal Trial proceedings for the Judgment of True Love.

And it is in the Universal Trial proceedings for the Judgment of True Love that a complete understanding of the formulation of the Absolute must be comprehended, to thereby provide Humankind with the Relativity needed to perfect their creation – and this will be "the Love of our Creator" establishing the Divine Entity of One Love.

CHAPTER ONE: THE ORIGINS OF OUR UNIVERSE

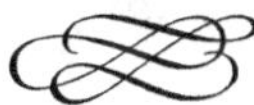

The Alpha, which is the Beginning process that conceived the development of Humankind's creation, began with the Origins of our Universe.

Verse 1

Now to begin, understand that our Creator is the Absolute Entity of our Universe, which means that the totality of our Universe is the complete Body of our Creator.

Verse 2

And within the Body of our Creator, there exists a "Creative Nature" (which is the most significant substance within our Universe); and this Creative Nature is called Love.

Verse 3

And Love is defined and expressed as the Desire to Need to Live.

Verse 4

And it is the expression of our Creator's Desire to Need to Live that produces Energy of all forms, and it is the Energies of our Creator's Desire to Need to Live that constitute within our Universe the Dimensions of our Creator's Spiritual Existence.

Verse 5

Wherein our Creator's Spiritual Existence functions as the Creative Force that creates and defines the Elements of our Universe.

Verse 6

But in relation to our Creator being the Absolute Entity of our Universe, it is our Creator's Spiritual Existence that is the Divine Entity of our Creator — because the Energies of our Creator's Desire to Need to Live will be the functioning of our Creator's Universal Existence.

Verse 7

And so from the Energies of our Creator's Desire to Need to Live, the origins of our Universe — which is the Life of our Creator — began with our Creator's Spiritual Existence giving meaning to the Divine Awareness of our Creator's Universal Atmosphere.

Section 1: The Divine Awareness of Our Creator's Universal Atmosphere

Verse 8

Now in essence, Life is defined as the awareness of a created existence; but in being the Absolute Entity of our Universe, in order for our Creator to distinguish what is Life "from" what is Not Life, the Negative and Positive polarities of the Energies of our Creator's Desire to Need to Live must be designated.

Verse 9

Because it is the polarities of the Negative and Positive that formulate the dimensions of our Creator's Mental State of Being aware of a Universal Atmosphere — wherein our Creator consciously differentiates what is Life from what is Not Life.

Verse 10

And being that in the Beginning there was only Darkness, to distinguish the Life of our Creator from what is Not the Life of our Creator, it was commanded, "Let There Be Light!"

Verse 11

And Light was produced by activating the Creative Energies of our Creator's Desire to Need to Live; and therefrom it was designated that:

(1) the Darkness (being the Creative Void to the Energies of our Creator's Desire to Need to Live) is the Negative polarity of our Creator's Universal Atmosphere, and

(2) the Light, being the Creative Force to the Energies of our Creator's Desire to Need to Live, is the Positive polarity of our Creator's Universal Atmosphere.

Verse 12

And from the Creative Energies of our Creator's Desire to Need to Live, the Activities that produced the Light had established a created awareness of the environmental surroundings that constitute the Mental and Physical composition of our Creator's Universal Existence; and from this Divine Awareness of our Creator's Universal Atmosphere, the Life of our Creator and the Origins of the Universe were conceived.

Section 2: Conceiving the Physics of Our Creator's Universal Existence

Verse 13

Now as the Darkness reflects the Negative polarization of our Creator's Universal Atmosphere and the Light reflects the Positive polarization of our Creator's Universal Atmosphere, the Life of our Creator was perceived by our Creator through the dimensions of our Creator's Mental State of being Conscious.

Verse 14

And upon distinguishing what is the Life of our Creator from what is Not the Life of our Creator, our Creator's Mental State of being Conscious began to process the Activities produced by the Creative Energies of our Creator's Desire to Need to Live.

Verse 15

And this processing of the Activities produced by the Creative Energies of our Creator's Desire to Need to Live was conspired through the series of actions, changes, and functions that brought about the experiences of a created existence in a course of Time that modulated within the Negative and Positive polarizations of our Creator's Universal Atmosphere.

Verse 16

And from this, the Science of Procreation was developed upon discovering that:

"In its chemical composition, the variance of applied Activity to the Creative Energies of our Creator's Desire to Need to Live will materialize the Elements that will compose the Properties of our Creator's Universal Existence."

Verse 17

Because:

• when the Creative Energies of our Creator's Desire to Need to Live were activated, Atomic Particles were ignited to produce the Light, in which manifested the Consciousness of our Creator's Existence;

• and when the Creative Energies of our Creator's Desire to Need to Live became deactivated, these Atomic Particles were formulated into Elements that defined the Spatial Contents of our Creator's Universal Atmosphere;

• and when the Creative Energies of our Creator's Desire to Need to Live were reactivated, those Elements were materialized into the Physical Properties that gave substance to the Physics of our Creator's Universal Existence.

Verse 18

And so from the study, observation, and application of the Science of Procreation, our Creator, in whom is the Absolute Entity of our Universe, had conceived the Physics of our Creator's Universal Existence within the dimensions of our Creator's Mental State of being Conscious as the Composition of the Elements, Interactions, Processes, and Principles to the Physical Properties that make up the Spatial Contents of the Universe.

Verse 19

And upon conceiving the Physics of our Creator's Universal Existence, our Creator's Spiritual Existence, which is the Divine Entity of our Creator, had developed the Desire to Need to Live "continuously" within the Spatial Contents of our Creator's Universal Atmosphere as our Creator's Light.

Verse 20

And therein were the Creative Energies of our Creator's Desire to Need to Live directed to procreate the Physical Properties of our Creator's Universal Existence within the Spatial Contents of our Creator's Universal Atmosphere, by materializing the Elements of our Creator's "Creative Nature" into the components needed for the Circuitry of our Creator's Light.

Section 3: Procreating the Physical Properties of our Creator's Universal Existence

Verse 21

Now in initiating the process of procreating the Physical Properties of our Creator's Universal Existence, the compounded substances that compose our Creator's "Creative Nature" were partitioned into three (3) Elements:

(1) the Authoritative Expression,

(2) the Reproductive Quality, and

(3) the Genetic Trait.

Verse 22

And these three (3) Elements of our Creator's "Creative Nature" were disseminated to materialize into the Components needed for our Creator's Light, wherein did:

(1) the Authoritative Expression of our Creator's "Creative

Nature" become the Electromotive Force that induces and measures the Positive Conductivity of our Universal Desire to Need to Live within the Physics that will sustain the illumination of our Creator's Light; and this dissemination procreated the Properties called God,

(2) *the Reproductive Quality of our Creator's "Creative Nature"* become the Electromagnetic Field that conducts and directs the Positive Energies of a Universal Desire to Need to Live with the Love of our Creator; and this dissemination procreated the Properties called Heaven, and

(3) *the Genetic Trait of our Creator's "Creative Nature"* become the Electrodynamics that retains and generates the activated Energies of our Creator's Desire to Need to Live within the Elements of the Universe; and this dissemination procreated the Properties called Earth.

Verse 23

And from this dissemination to the Elements of our Creator's "Creative Nature", the Electromotive Force, Electromagnetic Field, and Electrodynamics were composed to function as the Components for our Creator's Light, while the combined procreated Properties of God, Heaven, and Earth became the actual Physical Properties of our Creator's Universal Existence.

Verse 24

But with the process of conceiving the Physics of our Creator's Universal Existence occurring within the dimensions of our Creator's Mental State of being Conscious, the actual procreation of the Physical Properties of our Creator's Universal Existence begotten by the Creative Force of our Creator's Desire to Need to Live within the Spatial Contents of our Creator's Universal Atmosphere – which produced a Nuclear Reaction that separated the Positive polarities of the Universe from the Negative polarities of the Universe, thereby materializing the Circuitry of our Creator's Light within the Spatial Expansion of our Creator's Universal Atmosphere.

Verse 25

And from this Nuclear Reaction, the Energy generated was concentrated into an Orbital Star; and the Creative Energies consumed to light our Creator's (entire) Universal Atmosphere for a short period of time were harnessed as the Power Source that will radiate a much smaller area within the Spatial Contents of our Creator's Universal Atmosphere for a much longer period of time.

Verse 26

And with this Orbital Star, radiation is emitted into our Creator's Universal Atmosphere – thereby propagating the waves of Light, Heat, Sound, and subatomic Particles of our Creator's Creative Energies onto the physical Properties of our Creator's Universal Existence, thereby nourishing the Physics of our Creator's Universal Existence with the Sustenances needed to produce and maintain Life.

Verse 27

And as a result of the Nuclear Reaction produced by the Creative Force of our Creator's Desire to Need to Live within the Spatial Contents of our Creator's Universal Atmosphere:

(1) *the Positive Polarities of the Universe* became the Solar Energy that "EXTRACTS" the Active Energies of our Creator's Desire to Need to Live; and it is the functioning Extraction of Solar Energy that will govern Universal Growth and Development within the Physics of our Creator's Universal Existence, as its Ruling effects will produce the Spectrum of Day within the physical Properties of our Creator's Universal Existence, and

(2) *the Negative Polarities of the Universe* became the Dark Energy that "RETRACTS" the Active Energies of our Creator's Desire to Need to Live; and it is the functioning Retraction of Dark Energy that will process Individual Progress and Independent Potential within the Physics of our Creator's Universal Existence, as its Ruling effects will produce the Obscurity of Night within the Physical Properties of our Creator's Universal Existence, and

(3) *the Spatial Expansion of our Creator's Universal Atmosphere* became the Gravitational Force that "ATTRACTS" the Chemical Energies of a Natural Desire to Need to Live with the Mechanical Energies of a Universal Desire to Need to Live; and it is the functioning Attraction of Gravity that will calibrate the Equilibrium of Life within the Physics of our

Creator's Universal Existence, as its Ruling effects will sustain the Principles of Universal Law within the Physical Properties of our Creator's Universal Existence.

Verse 28

And it is the completed procreation of the physical Properties of our Creator's Universal Existence that manifests the Circuitry of our Creator's Light.

Section 4: The Circuitry of Our Creator's Light

Verse 29

The Circuitry of our Creator's Light is the designed configuration of the procreated Properties of God, Heaven, and Earth being electromagnetically "CONNECTED" to provide an uninterrupted path for Electrical Energy to illuminate our Creator's Light within the Spatial Contents of our Creator's Universal Atmosphere.

Verse 30

And in conforming with the Principles of Universal Law, the electromagnetic interaction within the Physics of our Creator's Universal Existence was configured to circuit the Love of our Creator as the induction that will direct the electrical flux within the Circuitry of our Creator's Light – as the Positive Energies of a Universal Desire to Need to Live "WITH" the Love of our Creator will produce the Electrical Current needed to illuminate our Creator's Light.

Verse 31

But for the purposes of distinguishing the Activities produced by the Creative Energies of our Creator's Desire to Need to Live within the Elements of the Universe – from – the Activities produced by the physical Properties of our Creator's Universal Existence, the Circuitry of our Creator's Light was designed to give the inhabitants of Earth the Free Will to independently express their Desire to Need to Live "WITH" the Love of our Creator.

Verse 32

Meaning that the illumination of our Creator's Light will depend upon the inhabitants of Earth's willingness to express either a Universal Desire to Need to Live with the Love of our Creator – or – a Universal Desire to Need to Live without the Love of our Creator.

Verse 33

Because it is from the Free Will expression exhibited by the inhabitants of Earth that will energize the Creative Energies of our Creator's Desire to Need to Live within the Elements of the Universe, thereby defining the "CLOSED" and "OPEN" Circuitry of our Creator's Light for the Power Surge to the Physics of our Creator's Universal Existence.

Subsection A: The Closed Circuitry of our Creator's Light
Verse 34

The Circuitry of our Creator's Light is Closed when the procreated Properties of Earth are electromagnetically "connected" with the procreated Properties of God and Heaven; meaning that the inhabitants of Earth are living in accordance with the Principles of Universal Law as authorized and governed by God and Heaven.

Verse 35

Whereby will the Conductivity to the Active Energies of our Creator's Desire to Need to Live within the Elements of the Universe become induced and measured by the procreated Properties of God and Heaven, to thereby generate and direct within the procreated Properties of Earth – the Positive Energies of a Universal Desire to Need to Live "with" the Love of our Creator.

Verse 36

Wherein will the Positive Energies produced by the physical Properties of our Creator's Universal Existence "ignite" the Radiance produced from Solar Energy, to thereby radiate the illumination of our Creator's Light.

Verse 37

Because the illumination of our Creator's Light is radiated when the Active Energies of our Creator's Desire to Need to Live within the Elements of the Universe are in cohesion with the Positive Energies of a Universal Desire to Need to Live with the Love of our Creator.

Verse 38

And as a result, the Positive Energies of a Universal Desire to Need to Live "with" the Love of our Creator will propel the Physics of our Creator's Universal Existence to operate within the Realities of a Positive Existence, and the Sustenance produced by the Radiant Energies of our Creator's Light will provide the inhabitants within the physical Properties of our Creator's Universal Existence with an Everlasting Life.

Subsection B: The Open Circuitry of our Creator's Light
Verse 39

The Circuitry of our Creator's Light is Open when the procreated Properties of Earth are electromagnetically "disconnected" from the procreated Properties of God and Heaven, meaning that the inhabitants of Earth are not living in accordance with the Principles of Universal Law as authorized and governed by God and Heaven.

Verse 40

Whereby grounding the Positive Energies of a Universal Desire to Need to Live "with" the Love of our Creator and inducing within the procreated Properties of Earth, the Negative Energies of a Universal Desire to Need to Live "without" the Love of our Creator.

Verse 41

And in the Open Circuitry of our Creator's Light, the Conductivity to the Active Energies of our Creator's Desire to Need to Live within the Elements of the Universe will in time become exhausted, as the Negative Energies of a Universal Desire to Need to Live "without" the Love of our Creator will cause the procreated Properties of Earth to function in a counter-productive manner.

Verse 42

And as a result, the physical Properties of our Creator's Universal Existence will operate within the Realities of a Negative Existence, and the Life-span for the inhabitants of Earth will sporadically expire due to the Physics of our Creator's Universal Existence not producing the Sustenance needed for Humankind to sustain an Everlasting Life.

Subsection C: The Power Surge to the Physics of our Creator's Universal Existence

Verse 43

But in completing the procreation to the physical Properties of our Creator's Universal Existence, the purpose of configuring the Open Circuitry for our Creator's Light was to Power Surge the Physics of our Creator's Universal Existence – thereby to stabilize the Closed Circuitry that will forever sustain the illumination of our Creator's Light.

Verse 44

Because in order to stabilize the Closed Circuitry that will forever sustain the Illumination of our Creator's Light, the inhabitants within the procreated Properties of Earth must electromagnetically "reconnect" with the procreated

Properties of God and Heaven – by willingly expressing the Universal Desire to Need to Live with the Love of our Creator.

Verse 45

And in order to truly express the Desire to Need to Live with the Love of our Creator, the inhabitants of Earth must first comprehend by experience – the Realities of a Negative Existence, whereby to then be given a Choice to either:

• *willingly choose to continue living "without" the Love of our Creator as the Crowned King of Heaven, or*

• *willingly choose to begin putting forth the effort needed to display the Desire to Need to Live "with" the Love of our Creator as the Crowned King of Heaven.*

Verse 46

And from this Choice to freely express a True Desire to Need to Live with the Love of our Creator, Humankind will execute the Power Surge needed to produce and sustain the Positive Energies that will forever illuminate our Creator's Light.

Verse 47

And therefore, it was designed that the following phase of development be taken to Power Surge the Physics of our Creator's Universal Existence:

(1) *Phase One:* for the purposes of Establishing the Closed Circuitry of our Creator's Light, the Love of our Creator was

perceived to conceive the origins of Humankind's creation as the Genetic inhabitants to the physical Properties of our Creator's Universal Existence; and this Phase is the application of the "Alpha".

(2) *Phase Two:* for the purposes of Perfecting Humankind's creation, the Spiritual Conflict between Good and Evil was engaged to Open the Circuitry of our Creator's Light, to thereby provide Humankind with the Free Will to express their True Desire to Need to Live with the Love of our Creator upon experiencing the Realities of a Negative Existence; and this Phase is the application of the "Omega".

(3) *Phase Three:* for the purposes of Completing the Procreation to the physical Properties of our Creator's Universal Existence, the Universal Trial proceedings for the Judgment of True Love were ordained to settle the Spiritual Conflict between Good and Evil – whereby to establish the One Love that will stabilize the Closed Circuitry that will forever sustain the illumination of our Creator's Light; and this Phase is the application of the "Absolute".

CHAPTER TWO: THE ORIGINS OF HUMANKIND'S CREATION

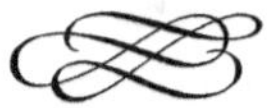

Verse 1

The Origins of Humankind's creation began with our Creator "perceiving" the Love of our Creator within the Circuitry of our Creator's Light, because in perception:

the Love of our Creator is the reflected Conduct and appreciated Livelihood of our Creator's Spiritual Existence within creation.

Verse 2

And in reference to the Circuitry of our Creator's Light, our Creator's Spiritual Existence within creation is perceived by our Creator—who is the Absolute Entity of our Universe—as the Positive Energies of our Creator's Desire to Need to Live within the Elements of the Universe.

Verse 3

And within the Circuitry of our Creator's Light:

(1) the reflected Conduct of the Positive Energies of our Creator's Desire to Need to Live within the Elements of the Universe became the Electrical Charge that powers our Creator's Light, and

(2) the appreciated Livelihood of the Positive Energies of our Creator's Desire to Need to Live within the Elements of the Universe became the Magnetic Force that illuminates our Creator's Light.

Verse 4

But in relation to Physics, our Creator's Spiritual Existence within creation is perceived by Creation as the procreated Properties of God – because within the Physics of our Creator's Universal Existence:

(1) the Conduct of the Positive Energies of our Creator's Desire to Need to Live within the Elements of the Universe becomes reflected within creation as the Image that will stabilize the Circuitry of our Creator's Light, and

(2) the Livelihood of the Positive Energies of our Creator's Desire to Need to Live within the Elements of the Universe becomes appreciated within creation as the Likeness that will sustain the Illumination of our Creator's Light.

Verse 5

And with the Image and Likeness of our Creator's Spiritual Existence within creation being perceived as the procreated

Properties of God, our Creator conceived the creation of Humankind from the procreated Properties of Earth—to thereby "embody" the Electrical Energies within the Circuitry of our Creator's Light.

Verse 6

Meaning that upon our Creator perceiving the Love of our Creator in relation to the Physics of our Creator's Universal Existence, Humankind became conceived as the Conductors of the Electrical Current needed to illuminate our Creator's Light.

Section 1: Conceiving Humankind's Creation

Verse 7

Now in conceiving the creation of Humankind, it was from the substances of the Earth that our Creator "formed" the body of the First Man created.

Verse 8

And from the Creative Energies of our Creator's Desire to Need to Live within the Elements of the Universe, Life was given to the First Man created.

Verse 9

And in the Beginning, this First Man created was the Love "of" our Creator as perceived by our Creator – because he "embodied" the reflected Conduct and appreciated

Livelihood to the Positive Energies of our Creator's Desire to Need to Live within the Elements of the Universe.

Verse 10

And therefrom the Heart and Rib of the First Man created, our Creator conceived Womankind; in whom became the Love "from" our Creator in relation to the Love of our Creator.

Verse 11

And from the relations of the First Man and Womankind, our Creator's Spiritual Existence was genetically reproduced within Humankind's creation as the activated Energies of Love.

Verse 12

And therein was our Creator's Spiritual Existence perceived by Humankind as the procreated Properties of God, because by definition – God is the Supreme Being of our Creator's Universal Existence; and with the First Man created being the Father of Humankind, he was the Person of God as the activated Energies of Love within Humankind's creation was the Essence of God.

Verse 13

And by Humankind perceiving the First Man created as the Person of God, while also perceiving the activated Energies of Love within Humankind's creation as the Essence of God – Humankind's creation was conceived to produce the

Positive Energies of a Universal Desire to Need to Live within the Physics that will illuminate our Creator's Light.

Section 2: Configuring the Circuitry that Illuminates our Creator's Light

Verse 14

Now, by conceiving the First Man created as the Person of God, the Electrical Current flow for the activated Energies of Love was designed to circulate in a Positive direction within Humankind's creation, to thereby electromagnetically connect the procreated Properties of Earth with the procreated Properties of God and Heaven.

Verse 15

Because instead of the Creative Energies of our Creator's Desire to Need to Live within the Elements of the Universe alternating from Negative to Positive within the polarities of the Universe, the Physics of our Creator's Universal Existence will maintain the Positive circulation to the activated Energies of Love – by Reciprocating within Humankind's creation, the Positive Energies of a Universal Desire to Need to Live with the Love of our Creator.

Verse 16

And from that Positive circulation to the activated Energies of Love, the reflected Conduct and appreciated Livelihood of our Creator's Spiritual Existence within Humankind's creation will circuit the Positive Electrical Energies that will energize our Creator's Desire to Need to Live within the Elements of the Universe.

Verse 17

But this reciprocation of Love can only be manifested by Humankind worshipping and obeying the Person of God in accordance with our Creator's Universal Laws of Existence.

Verse 18

Because by definition, our Creator's Universal Laws of Existence are the established Principles that maintain the proper Code of Conduct in which to sustain the Conditional Realities of our Creator's Spiritual Existence within creation.

Verse 19

And from Humankind worshipping and obeying the Person of God in accordance with our Creator's Universal Laws of Existence, the activated Energies of Love will remain in constant activation within the embodiment of Humankind's creation – to thereby sustain the illumination of our Creator's Light, which in turn will maintain Humankind's Everlasting Life.

Verse 20

Which means that when Humankind displays their Desire to Need to Live with the Love of our Creator by obeying the Person of God in accordance with our Creator's Universal Laws of Existence, our Creator will reciprocate his Desire to

Need to Live within the Elements of the Universe by producing and emitting the Sustenance that maintains Everlasting Life.

Verse 21

Because by worshipping and obeying the Person of God in accordance with our Creator's Universal Laws of Existence, Humankind will stimulate the Pleasures of our Creator's Spiritual Existence within their creation – whereby exalting our Creator's Glory; which in turn energizes the Creative Energies of our Creator's Desire to Need to Live within the Elements of the Universe.

Verse 22

But in configuring the Circuitry that illuminates our Creator's Light, it was the First Man created whose Livelihood as the Person of God was to be appreciated by Humankind as the established Authority of our Creator's Spiritual Existence within creation.

Verse 23

And as the established Authority of our Creator's Spiritual Existence within creation, the First Man created sat upon our Creator's Throne as the Crowned King of Heaven – to thereby rule the Physics of our Creator's Universal Existence, by keeping charge and the course for the Positive Conductivity of a Universal Desire to Need to Live within the Physics that sustains the illumination of our Creator's Light.

Section 3: Prescribing the Perfection of Humankind's Creation

Verse 24

Now, in the Beginning times of Humankind's existence, the Closed Circuitry that was initially established to illuminate our Creator's Light was not Stable because Humankind's creation was not Perfected.

Verse 25

Meaning that due to Humankind being conceived within the Realities of a Positive Existence, the Physics of our Creator's Universal Existence was unable to sustain the illumination of our Creator's Light because Humankind did not go through the process of overcoming their Imperfections.

Verse 26

And Humankind's Imperfections are the Evil impurities that exist within the nature of their creation, which emerged into activity upon Humankind not having an "Objective Understanding of the Relativity of God."

Verse 27

And by not having an Objective Understanding of the Relativity of God, in time, Humankind began to take the Goodness of God for granted – and as a result, Humankind began violating our Creator's Universal Laws of Existence, which in turn propelled our Creator's Spiritual Existence to abandon the embodiment of Humankind's creation.

Verse 28

And as the Conductivity to the activated Energies of our Creator's Desire to Need to Live within the Elements of the Universe became exhausted within Humankind's creation, due to Humankind not properly reciprocating the Desire to Need to Live with the Love of our Creator – our Creator's Light had ceased to illuminate and the physical Properties of our Creator's Universal Existence began to operate within the Realities of a Negative Existence.

Verse 29

But being that our Creator is All-Knowing, our Creator had designed the Open Circuitry of our Creator's Light as the Second Phase of Development – to thereby institute the undertaking course that will give Humankind an Objective Understanding of the Relativity of God, whereas to allow Humankind to overcome their Imperfections.

Verse 30

Because upon conceiving Humankind's creation, it was understood that in order for Humankind to overcome their Imperfections – Humankind must first experience the Conductivity of Evil while living within the Realities of a Negative Existence, to thereby Redirect the Conductivity to the activated Energies of Love in the direction that will "Power Surge" the Physics of our Creator's Universal Existence.

Verse 31

And from this Power Surge, the Positive Conductivity to the activated Energies of Love will stabilize the Closed Circuitry that will forever sustain the illumination of our Creator's Light, whereby allowing the physical Properties of our Creator's Universal Existence to permanently operate within the Realities of a Positive Existence; and this will be the Third Phase of Development for the Circuitry of our Creator's Light.

Verse 32

But it is in overcoming the Imperfections of Humankind's creation, will Humankind be created in the Image and after the Likeness of God; in which is our Creator's process of developing the Perfection of Humankind's creation through a Universal Trial proceeding that will evaluate Humankind's Desire to Need to Live with the Love of our Creator as the Crowned King of Heaven.

Verse 33

And therefore, in Prescribing the Perfection of Humankind's creation, Humankind must completely understand the Relativity of God – Subjectively and Objectively.

Subsection A: Understanding the Relativity of God
Verse 34

The Relativity of God is Humankind's comprehension of the value and significance that the actual Person of God has in connection with Humankind's existence and well-being.

Verse 35

And in the Beginning times of Humankind's existence, living within our Creator's Universal Existence was All Good because the Person of God – in whom was the First Man created – sat upon our Creator's Throne as the Crowned King of Heaven.

Verse 36

And it was his value as the Crowned King of Heaven which allowed our Creator's Spiritual Blessings to be bestowed upon Humankind's creation in a prescribed order that supplied Humankind's existence with the Sustenances needed for an Everlasting Life.

Verse 37

And with Humankind worshipping and obeying the Person of God in accordance with our Creator's Universal Laws of Existence, any and all lawsuits and/or legal claims that were filed and reported within our Creator's Universal Existence were presented to and/or reviewed by our Creator's Omnipotent Court of Universal Law; in which it was the duty of the Crowned King of Heaven to oversee and preside over as the Chief Justice of our Creator's Omnipotent Court of Universal Law.

Verse 38

And it was his significance as the Chief Justice of our Creator's Omnipotent Court of Universal Law which upheld

World Peace and Order for Humankind's well-being living within our Creator's Universal Existence.

Verse 39

And it was in being the Crowned King of Heaven and by fulfilling the duties of the Chief Justice of our Creator's Omnipotent Court of Universal Law, that gave meaning to the Person of God's value and significance in connection with Humankind's existence and well-being – thereby defining the Relativity of God.

Verse 40

But in the Beginning, due to Humankind not having an Objective Understanding of the Relativity of God, Humankind did not comprehend the effects of Evil or what it meant to Die – because in living within the Realities of a Positive Existence, there was No Evil being done and Humankind did not Die.

Verse 41

And in its actuality, not having an Objective Understanding of the Relativity of God meant that:

(1) Humankind did not have an actual realistic comprehension of the Consequences of not worshipping and obeying the Person of God in accordance with our Creator's Universal Laws of Existence – other than what the Person of God had stated and explained to them, and

(2) Humankind did not have an actual realistic comprehension of the Reality of living without the Person of God as the established Authority of our Creator's Spiritual Existence within creation.

Verse 42

And by Humankind not having an Objective Understanding of the Relativity of God, in time Humankind started to take the Person of God for granted because Humankind "ignorantly" figured that once Life was given to them – an Everlasting Life was perpetual, whereby there was no need to continue to worship and obey the Person of God; and this way of thinking led Humankind to begin violating our Creator's Universal Laws of Existence.

Verse 43

And although Humankind did not have an Objective Understanding of the Relativity of God, Humankind in the Beginning did have a Subjective Understanding of the Relativity of God – which meant that Humankind worshipped and obeyed the Person of God in accordance with our Creator's Universal Laws of Existence because it was the proper order of living and that it was what they were taught to do, due to there being No other concept of living at that time.

Verse 44

But in time, Humankind began to develop Questions concerning the restrictions that were placed in adhering to our Creator's Universal Laws of Existence – in which many of those questions were answered with a "Because God says so -or- Because God says Not to."

Verse 45

And due to Humankind's creation being conceived within the Realities of a Positive Existence, Humankind was without the actual experience which would validate the Reasoning that would explain why there are certain restrictions placed upon our living within our Creator's Universal Existence.

Verse 46

Because in the Beginning times of Humankind's existence, Humankind's comprehension level was in an adolescent stage; and as an example:

• "Just like when Parents tell their Children not to play with Fire or they will get burnt, if the children do not know what the actual consequences and reality of being burnt means – then the Children are not going to completely understand Why Not to play with Fire."

Verse 47

And in the Beginning times of Humankind's existence, it was to no avail for God to provide Humankind with a comprehension of Dying – without the actual experienced "Reasoning" of the Death that will occur as a result of violating our Creator's Universal Laws of Existence.

Verse 48

And by Humankind only having a Subjective Understanding of the Relativity of God, it was as if the Person of God was using Threats to force Humankind to worship and obey him.

Verse 49

And Humankind being forced to worship and obey the Person of God is not a proper expression of the Positive Energies needed to reciprocate our Creator's Desire to Need to Live within the Elements of the Universe.

Verse 50

Because in the manner of being Threatened or Forced, Humankind does not have the Free Will to express and display their true Desire to Need to Live with the Love of our Creator.

Verse 51

And by Humankind not having the Free Will to express and display their True Love for the Person of God, the Positive Expression of a Universal Desire to Need to Live with the Love of our Creator was not established and the Person of God was unable to determine if Humankind truly loved and appreciated him or just loved the Spiritual Blessings that were bestowed upon their creation.

Verse 52

Wherefore, by Humankind only having a Subjective Understanding of the Relativity of God – the problems pertaining to Not having an Objective Understanding of the Relativity of God became apparent within Humankind's "willingness" to honor and obey our Creator's Sacred Rites of Marriage.

Subsection B: Our Creator's Sacred Rites of Marriage

Verse 53

Our Creator's Sacred Rites of Marriage are our Creator's prescribed ceremonial order and customary form for worshipping God in accordance with our Creator's Universal Laws of Existence.

Verse 54

And although to worship God in accordance with our Creator's Universal Laws of Existence means to display the Desire to Need to Live with the Love of our Creator, it is the activities of Sex that were specifically designed by our Creator to be the celebrated custom for displaying the Desire to Need to Live with the Love of our Creator.

Verse 55

But in order to engage in the activities of Sex and properly worship God in accordance with our Creator's Universal Laws of Existence, Humankind must adhere to our Creator's Sacred Rites of Marriage – because by displaying the Desire to Need to Live with the Love of our Creator through the activities of Sex, this custom "exalts our Creator's Glory" and allows Humankind to receive our Creator's Spiritual Blessings as a reciprocation to our

Creator's Desire to Need to Live within the Elements of the Universe.

Verse 56

And by definition:

(1) our Creator's Glory is the stimulated Pleasures of our Creator's Spiritual Existence within creation, and

(2) our Creator's Spiritual Blessings are the intensified sensations and favored prosperities that are transmitted by our Creator's Glory to Humankind's creation.

Verse 57

And it is in adhering to our Creator's Sacred Rites of Marriage that each person, before engaging in the activities of Sex, must first become Blessed – In Marriage with the Love of our Creator.

Verse 58

Which means that before engaging in the activities of Sex, each person must initially submit their Vows to God in the Virtuous Order that is authorized and prescribed by the Authorities of our Creator's Throne.

Verse 59

Because by adhering to our Creator's Sacred Rites of Marriage, Humankind is restricted from having Unmarital and Adulterated Sex – whereas to allow the Sustenance needed for an Everlasting Life to properly flow from our

Creator's Throne to Humankind's creation in the prescribed Order of Virtue as established by the Authorities of our Creator's Throne.

Verse 60

But let it be understood that it is not the activities of Sex in which the Sustenance that provides Humankind with an Everlasting Life – it is our Creator's Spiritual Blessings and the Radiant Energies of our Creator's Light that are the Sustenance that provides Humankind with an Everlasting Life.

Verse 61

Whereinto, it is worshipping God through the activities of Sex – to thereby exalt our Creator's Glory, that is the Medium which transmits the Sustenance that provides Humankind with an Everlasting Life.

Verse 62

Because worshipping God through the activities of Sex as established by our Creator's Sacred Rites of Marriage stimulates the Pleasures of our Creator's Spiritual Existence within creation – whereby energizing the Creative Energies of our Creator's Desire to Need to Live within the Elements of the Universe, which in turn energizes the Metabolism Elements that regenerate the Physics within Humankind's creation.

Subsection C: Taking the Goodness of God for Granted
Verse 63

Now these problems pertaining to Humankind not having an Objective Understanding of the Relativity of God began to emerge when People became "curious" and thought that Humankind did not need the Person of God to receive our Creator's Spiritual Blessings.

Verse 64

Because some People "ignorantly" figured that there was no need for a Virtuous Order to be prescribed when the Pleasures deriving from Sex are the Sustenance that provides Humankind with an Everlasting Life.

Verse 65

Whereinto did those People think that by just engaging in the activities of Sex, they could receive our Creator's Spiritual Blessings and maintain an Everlasting Life without the Person of God – which is basically taking the Goodness of God for granted.

Verse 66

Because by definition, taking the Goodness of God for Granted means that a Person does not Respect the Code of Conduct or Appreciate the Livelihood of the Person of God – but yet, desires to benefit from the Blessings and Pleasures deriving from our Creator's Spiritual Existence.

Verse 67

And as Humankind began to Multiply upon the Earth, the People became bolder and their questions to God turned into the questioning of God's Authority – which subsequently led People to disobey the Person of God and violate our Creator's Universal Laws of Existence.

Verse 68

And as Humankind continued to violate our Creator's Universal Laws of Existence, the Conductivity to the activated Energies of Love began to degenerate with Humankind's disrespectful actions – and as a result of Humankind taking the Goodness of God for Granted, the Pleasures of our Creator's Spiritual Existence ceased being stimulated within Humankind's creation.

Verse 69

Because by violating our Creator's Universal Laws of Existence, Humankind proceeded in inducing the Negative Energies of a Universal Desire to Need to Live without the Love of our Creator as the Crowned King of Heaven – thereby no longer exalting our Creator's Glory.

Verse 70

And as a result of not exalting our Creator's Glory, the Physics of our Creator's Universal Existence no longer generated the Positive Energies needed to illuminate our Creator's Light and consequently – Death became a Reality as the physical Properties of our Creator's Universal Existence began to operate within the Realities of a Negative Existence.

Verse 71

But in order to create Humankind in the Image and "after" the Likeness of God, our Creator had to allow Humankind to take the Goodness of God for Granted, to thereby provide Humankind with an objective understanding of the Relativity of God – because in allowing Humankind to experience the Realities of a Negative Existence, Humankind is given the opportunity to overcome the Imperfections of their creation; and this is our Creator Prescribing the Perfection of Humankind's creation.

CHAPTER THREE: INITIATING THE SPIRITUAL CONFLICT BETWEEN GOOD AND EVIL

The Omega, which is the ending process that perceives the development of Humankind's creation, began with initiating the Spiritual Conflict between Good and Evil.

Verse 1

Now, in the beginning, before Humankind began to violate our Creator's Universal Laws of Existence, our Creator knew that Humankind's creation was not made in perfection – whereas upon conceiving Humankind's creation, it was prescribed that Humankind must overcome their imperfections, to thereby be made in the Image and after the Likeness of God.

Verse 2

And by definition:

(1) The Image of God is the reflection of Righteous Conduct, and

(2) The Likeness of God is the appreciation of a Virtuous Livelihood.

Verse 3

But due to Humankind's creation being conceived within the Realities of a Positive Existence, in order for our Creator to create Humankind in the Image and after the Likeness of God, Humankind must experience the Realities of a Negative Existence, to thereby overcome their own Imperfections.

Verse 4

Because by definition, being created in the Image and after the Likeness of God is our Creator's process of developing the Perfection of Humankind's creation, in which Humankind must overcome their Imperfections by subduing the Energies of a Negative Existence – to thereby be made capable of sustaining the Energies of a Positive Existence.

Verse 5

And to create Humankind in the Image and after the Likeness of God, our Creator permitted Humankind's imperfections to induce the Negative Energies of a Universal Desire to Need to Live "without" the Love of our Creator as the Crowned King of Heaven – thereby producing the Realities of a Negative Existence.

And this undertaking course of action taken by our Creator to allow Humankind to experience the Realities of a

Negative Existence, to thereby overcome their Imperfections, came to become the Spiritual Conflict between Good and Evil.

Verse 7

And by definition, the Spiritual Conflict between Good and Evil is the power clash of a Universal Will to establish the understandings that distinguish a Positive Existence from a Negative Existence.

Verse 8

And in correlation with the Power surge to the physics of our Creator's Universal Existence (refer to Chapter One, verse 43 - verse 48), the Spiritual Conflict between Good and Evil became the undertaking course taken to stabilize the Closed Circuitry Cthat will forever sustain the illumination of our Creator's Light.

Verse 9

Because within its actualities, the Due Process of settling the Spiritual Conflict between Good and Evil will allow Humankind to perceive the development of their creation – to thereby become perfected upon receiving an objective understanding of the Relativity of God, whereby will Humankind be created in the Image and after the Likeness of God.

Verse 10

And therefore, to institute the undertaking course to establish the understandings that distinguish a Positive Existence from a Negative Existence, our Creator had created an Angel known to Humankind as Satan, to be God's adversary, in whom will initiate the Spiritual Conflict between Good and Evil; as he (Satan) was predestined to represent the Universal Will of Evil.

Verse 11

And as an Angel, Satan was a unique creation, who, like the First Man created, was "formed" from the substances of the Earth – but the Creative Energies of our Creator's Desire to Need to Live within the Elements of the Universe did not give Satan life, and instead, our Creator generated Satan's existence from the Retractive energies of a Universal Desire to Need to Live as the Absolute (also known as Dark Energy).

Section 1: Satan's Legal Claim and Argument

Verse 12

Now, in the beginning, when Humankind was living within the Realities of a Positive Existence, Satan was the most influential Angel within the Kingdom of Heaven – whose duties were to establish the substantiated meaning to our Creator's Glory.

Verse 13

Which basically meant that Satan was like the Minister for Love, because he was in charge of giving meaning to the sensations and prosperities that were transmitted to Humankind's creation from the stimulated pleasures of our Creator's Spiritual Existence.

Verse 14

But upon realizing the significance of his creation, Satan soon became excessively proud of his accomplishments and appearance – and due to Humankind not having an objective understanding of the Relativity of God, Satan soon developed the desire to be worshipped like God.

Verse 15

But as established by our Creator's Sacred Rites of Marriage, in order to generate the energies that propel the Realities of a Positive Existence – only the Love of our Creator is to be worshipped within the physical properties of our Creator's Universal Existence.

Verse 16

And so, in his attempts to contest the Love of our Creator, Satan had used his position and influence within the Kingdom of Heaven to make the Claim that:

"Living in accordance with an Unconditional Law of existing would be 'more pleasurable' than living in accordance with our Creator's Universal Laws of Existence."

Verse 17

And by definition, living in accordance with an Unconditional Law of existing means that there should be no requirements or obligations needed to fulfill the performance, completion, or existence of what is committed or established in the name of Love and Righteousness or that which is Morally Right.

Verse 18

And upon presenting his Claim to our Creator's Omnipotent Court of Universal Law, Satan made the argument that:

"An Unconditional Law of existing would allow Humankind to experience unlimited gratification, to thereby fulfill the increasing desires of our Creator's Spiritual Existence within creation."

Verse 19

Because specifically, Satan believed that the stimulated Pleasures of our Creator's Spiritual Existence within Humankind's creation would increase by allowing Humankind to experience the gratifications of Sex without all the "conditions and restrictions" established by our Creator's Universal Laws of Existence.

Verse 20

And by allowing Humankind to fulfill their own individual sexual desires without conditions and restrictions, the summation of everyone enjoying the stimulated Pleasures of our Creator's Spiritual Existence within their creation will not only be more satisfying to Humankind – but also more fulfilling to our Creator's Spiritual Existence as the Divine Entity of our Creator, due to the fact that our Creator's Spiritual Existence exists within Humankind's creation as the activated Energies of Love.

Verse 21

And so, for the reason of fulfilling the increasing desires of our Creator's Spiritual Existence within creation, it was Satan's Claim that living in accordance with an Unconditional Law of existing would be "more pleasurable" than living in accordance with our Creator's Universal Laws of Existence.

Section 2: The Disposition of our Creator's Omnipotent Court of Universal Law

Verse 22

Now when Satan's Claim was originally heard by the Chief Justice of our Creator's Omnipotent Court of Universal Law, it was explained to Satan that in order for Humankind to live in accordance with an Unconditional Law of existing – that would mean to live "without" the need for the Love of our Creator to be the established Authority of our Creator's Spiritual Existence within creation.

Verse 23

And "without" the Love of our Creator as the established Authority of our Creator's Spiritual Existence within creation, Humankind cannot be bestowed with our Creator's Spiritual Blessings in the prescribed Virtuous Order that will maintain Humankind's Everlasting Life.

Verse 24

Because understand:

(1) Our Creator's Spiritual Blessings are the sensations and prosperities that are transmitted by our Creator's Glory to Humankind's creation, and

(2) Our Creator's Glory is the stimulated Pleasures of our Creator's Spiritual Existence within creation, and

(3) In order for Humankind to be bestowed with our Creator's Spiritual Blessings, Humankind must become Blessed-In Marriage with the Love of our Creator, and

(4) The Love of our Creator is the Person of God in whom sits upon our Creator's Throne as the Crowned King of Heaven, and

(5) Becoming Blessed-In Marriage with the Love of our Creator will permit Humankind to receive our Creator's Spiritual Blessings from our Creator's Throne in the prescribed Virtuous Order that will maintain Humankind's Everlasting Life.

Verse 25

And furthermore, maintaining the prescribed Virtuous Order of Humankind receiving our Creator's Spiritual Blessings is the very reason why there are Conditions and Restrictions established by our Creator's Universal Laws of Existence in the form of our Creator's Sacred Rites of Marriage.

Verse 26

Because it is in accordance with our Creator's Sacred Rites of Marriage that:

(1) Upon becoming Blessed-In Marriage with the Love of our Creator, Humankind will be directed to engage in our Creator's celebrated custom for worshipping God, and

(2) Engaging in our Creator's celebrated custom for worshipping God is exhibited through the activities of Sex, and

(3) Humankind worshipping God through the activities of Sex exalts our Creator's Glory, and

(4) The exalting of our Creator's Glory is the Activating Force in which stimulates the Pleasures of our Creator's Spiritual Existence within Humankind's creation, and

(5) Upon the exalting of our Creator's Glory, the stimulated Pleasures of our Creator's Spiritual Existence will transmit to Humankind's creation – the sensations and prosperities that are equivalent to the Value of each person's Virtues, and

(6) These sensations and prosperities, which are our Creator's Spiritual Blessings – are the Sustenances that will energize the Metabolism Element within the Physics of Humankind's creation, whereby to maintain Humankind's Everlasting Life, but

(7) If any person should engage in the activities of Sex without the authorization prescribed by our Creator's Sacred Rites of Marriage, the Pleasures of our Creator's Spiritual Existence will not be stimulated within their creation – and as a result, the activated Energies of Love will degenerate and will not remain in constant activation within their embodiment.

Verse 27

Wherefore, authorizing the prescribed Virtuous Order of Humankind receiving our Creator's Spiritual Blessings is the very reason why Humankind "Need" the Love of our Creator to be the established Authority of our Creator's Spiritual Existence within creation.

Verse 28

And as established by our Creator's Sacred Rites of Marriage, it is in authorizing the prescribed Virtuous Order of Humankind receiving our Creator's Spiritual Blessings – must every person before becoming Blessed-In Marriage with the Love of our Creator assess within their creation, the Virtuous Capacity for the activated Energies of Love.

Verse 29

Because understand:

(1) The Virtuous Capacity for the activated Energies of Love is the measured Value of a person's Virtues, as ascertained by that person's accumulative Will-Power to validate the Conditional Realities of our Creator's Spiritual Existence within their creation, and

(2) The Conditional Realities of our Creator's Spiritual Existence are the actual Righteous Qualities and Moral Behavior in which capacitates the Virtues that allow the activated Energies of Love to remain in constant activation within the embodiment of Humankind's creation, and

(3) By validating the Conditional Realities of our Creator's Spiritual Existence within a person's creation, the Value of that person's Virtues will be dutifully assessed – whereby establishing the qualifications needed to verify that person's Potentials and prove their Worthiness to handle and receive the Spiritual Blessings that our Creator will bestow upon them; and this also includes those Anointed to sit upon our Creator's Throne.

Verse 30

And upon assessing within their creation, the Virtuous Capacity for the activated Energies of Love – each person will then become occupationally placed within the designed configuration that induces the Positive Energies needed to sustain the illumination of our Creator's Light.

Verse 31

Because understand, within the Physics of our Creator's Universal Existence:

(1) Our Creator's Spiritual Blessings are capacitated into (2) two Virtuous forms:

A. Spiritual Blessings of Glory – in which are reserved for those people who occupy within the Kingdom of Heaven as Crowns of Glory, and

B. Spiritual Blessings of Grace – in which are reserved for those people who occupy within the Kingdoms of the Earth as Crowns of Life, and

(2) Within each Virtuous form of our Creator's Spiritual Blessings, there are various degrees of Magnetic Force, which rank and characterize a person's Potential to stimulate the Pleasures of our Creator's Spiritual Existence within their creation, and

(3) It is the contained Magnetic Force that distinguishes a person's Worth and Ability to retain the Intensified sensations and Favored prosperities that are received from our Creator's Spiritual Blessings.

Verse 32

And in correlation with the Components for our Creator's Light:

(1) It is the stimulated Pleasures of our Creator's Spiritual Existence within Humankind's creation that establish the

Electromotive Force that induces and measures the Positive Conductivity needed to sustain the Illumination of our Creator's Light, and

(2) It is the validated Conditional Realities of our Creator's Spiritual Existence within Humankind's creation that establish the Electromagnetic Field that generates and directs the Positive Energies needed to stabilize the Circuitry of our Creator's Light, and

(3) It is the Sequential Rankings and the Status Characterization of our Creator's Spiritual Blessings that establish the Electrodynamics that electromagnetically connect the procreated Properties of God and Heaven with the procreated Properties of Earth.

Verse 33

Wherefore, sustaining the illumination of our Creator's Light for Humankind's Everlasting Life is the very reason why a Virtuous Order of Humankind receiving our Creator's Spiritual Blessings must be prescribed and authorized by the established Authority of our Creator's Spiritual Existence within creation.

Verse 34

And for the ascribed reasons, it is the Disposition of our Creator's Omnipotent Court of Universal Law that – living in accordance with an Unconditional Law of existing "would Not be More Pleasurable" than living in accordance with our Creator's Universal Laws of Existence.

Section 3: Satan's Rebuttal and Motion for a Change of Venue

Verse 35

Now in rebuttal, Satan contested that no one should have to prove their worthiness to receive our Creator's Spiritual Blessings because that would be a form of exploitation.

Verse 36

And instead, our Creator's Spiritual Blessings should be bestowed upon Humankind's creation in accordance with the needs of a person's sexual desires, and Humankind should not be limited from experiencing the gratifications of Sex by adhering to conditions and restrictions.

Verse 37

Because, as argued by Satan, if worshipping God is about displaying the Desire to Need to Live with the Love of our Creator, then Humankind should stimulate the Pleasures of our Creator's Spiritual Existence by satisfying the needs of their own sexual desires due to the fact that our Creator's Spiritual Existence exists within Humankind's creation as the activated Energies of Love.

Verse 38

And this argument is the motive behind why Satan made the Claim that living in accordance with an Unconditional Law of existing would be "more pleasurable" than living in accordance with our Creator's Universal Laws of Existence.

Verse 39

But our Creator's Omnipotent Court of Universal Law had rejected Satan's Claim that living in accordance with an Unconditional Law of existing would be "more pleasurable" than living in accordance with our Creator's Universal Laws of Existence, and stated that said Claim lacks merit and is based on unfounded theory.

Verse 40

And thereupon, the Court rejecting Satan's Claim, Satan objected to the grounds that his Claim lacks merit and proceeded to Motion the Court for a Change of Venue, whereby stating that the Court's decision to reject his Claim was prejudice due to the fact that – if said Claim questions the Relativity of God, then the Claim also challenges the jurisdictions of our Creator's Omnipotent Court of Universal Law with the Person of God presiding as Chief Justice over said Claim.

Verse 41

And thereafter, Satan's objection and Motion for a Change of Venue, the Person of God had rebuked Satan's Claim and declared that the underlying truth was that Satan wanted to do whatever he wanted without restrictions – and that Satan's Claim was actually an inclination of him becoming defiant.

Verse 42

And this rebuke of Satan's Claim provoked Satan to accuse

the Person of God of making restrictions that limit the potentials of other creations so that no one else can prove to be more worthy of sitting upon our Creator's Throne, namely him.

Verse 43

And it was by Satan's request that an Appeal of Satan's Claim be presented to the Angels of Heaven, in whom were women whose duties were to uphold the exalting of our Creator's Glory – because, as stated by Satan, it is Womankind who hold the true power to decide who to have sex with and that this power should not be dictated by the Person of God, whereas it should be a Woman's prerogative to choose who she should have sexual relations with.

Verse 44

And in response to Satan's request, our Creator's Omnipotent Court was in agreement with Womankind having the Free Will to choose who to have sex with, but also added that Womankind's decision must also coincide with having the Free Will to Desire to Need to Live "with" or "without" the Love of our Creator as the established Authority of our Creator's Spiritual Existence within creation.

Verse 45

And therefore, it was decided by our Creator's Omnipotent Court of Universal Law that Satan's Motion for a Change of

Venue be granted and that an Appeal to Satan's Claim be presented to the Angels of Heaven; and as it was noted on record that Satan was challenging the Person of God for rights to sit upon our Creator's Throne – it was "with" the Court's Decision to grant Satan's Motion for a Change of Venue that the Person of God was on record accepting Satan's challenge for rights to sit upon our Creator's Throne.

Section 4: Satan's Appeal to the Angels of Heaven

Verse 46

Now, it was Satan's Appeal to the Angels of Heaven which gave Satan a platform to publicly challenge the Person of God for rights to sit upon our Creator's Throne.

Verse 47

And in pertinent to Satan's Claim that living in accordance with an Unconditional Law of existing would be "more pleasurable" than living in accordance with our Creator's Universal Law of Existence – Satan's Appeal presented the Angels of Heaven with (3) three allegations:

(1) Satan's first allegation accused the Person of God of misleading and coercing Humankind into believing that by not worshipping the Person of God through the activities of Sex, the activating Energies of Love will not perform properly within the physics of Humankind's creation and as a result, Humankind will Surely Die – as it was contested by

Satan that the Pleasures of our Creator's Spiritual Existence are stimulated from each person's own Desire to Need to Live and by satisfying their own sexual desires, the gratifying sensations thereof will perform exceedingly more pleasurable within Humankind's creation continuously.

(2) Satan's second allegation accused God of alluring the Angels of Heaven into unknowingly falsifying the capabilities and strengths of the Person of God, because there was no factual proof or evidence to show how the Person of God actually earned the right to sit upon our Creator's Throne – as it was contested by Satan that the Person of God was pretentious and his qualifications were fallacious due to the fact that his Authority to sit upon our Creator's Throne was given to him only because of Birthright.

(3) Satan's third allegation accused God of making restrictions and marital laws to conceal the Person of God's impotence and inability to fulfill the duties required in upholding the Power needed to sit upon our Creator's Throne – as it was contested by Satan that the Person of God, who is the actual embodied creation of our Creator's Spiritual Existence, in the growth of Humankind's created development, is relatively invalid and that there are better-qualified creations to represent the power that sits upon our Creator's Throne.

Verse 48

And upon presenting these allegations, Satan made the argument that Humankind should not have to prove to be worthy of our Creator's Spiritual Blessings – especially since the Person of God has not proven worthy to sit upon our Creator's Throne.

Verse 49

And furthermore, Humankind should have the freedom to worship God however they choose to express their Desire to Need to Live – because why should Humankind worshiping God be directed towards "pleasing" the Person of God when we should focus on "pleasing" the Essence of God due to the fact that our Creator's Spiritual Existence is the greater Entity that exists within all of Humankind's creation.

Verse 50

And with the Appeal, Satan campaigned that he should represent the Power of our Creator's Throne – whereby he will give everyone the freedom to worship God as they please.

Verse 51

And as campaigned by Satan, if the activities of Sex are what stimulate the Pleasures of our Creator's Spiritual Existence within Humankind's creation – whereby to illuminate our Creator's Light, then Humankind should be able to have Sex with whomever, however, and whenever they choose to express Love.

Verse 52

And from Satan's Appeal to the Angels of Heaven, the litigations to settle the Spiritual Conflict between Good and Evil began.

CHAPTER FOUR: INSTITUTING THE DUE PROCESS OF SETTLING THE SPIRITUAL CONFLICT BETWEEN GOOD AND EVIL

Verse 1

Now, although Satan was manipulating the Truth and blatantly accusing the Person of God of lying to the People, the Person of God made No Response to the Allegations or Arguments made within Satan's Appeal to the Angels of Heaven—because the Person of God's Legal Stance was already established with the Disposition of our Creator's Omnipotent Court of Universal Law.

Verse 2

And because those Allegations were presented as a Legal Claim, by Due Process of Universal Law, our Creator knew that before He could punish Satan for making such Allegations, the Person of God had to first prove to the People that the Allegations made against him were False— and remaining Silent to Satan's Appeal was strategic because, in order to prove that the Allegations were bogus, He had to allow the Cause and Effects of Sin to take its course.

Verse 3

And although the People were bewildered by the Allegations made against God, along with God's lack of response to the Allegations—when Satan's Appeal was deliberated by the Angels of Heaven, there were Angels who did not agree with Satan because there was No corroborating evidence supporting Satan's Allegations against the Person of God.

Verse 4

But in all righteousness, they also could not disagree with Satan because Humankind did not objectively understand the Relativity of God, due to Humankind not being given a True Free Will to worship God—and by Universal Law, Humankind must not be Forced to worship God.

Verse 5

And it was stated that in order to truly understand which way of "Living" is More Pleasurable, Humankind should be given a Choice through Experience to choose whether to worship God in accordance with our Creator's Universal Laws of Existence or in accordance with an Unconditional Law of existing.

Verse 6

And because the idea of a More Pleasurable living with Womankind having the right to choose their own sexual relations was intriguing—the Concept of living in accordance with an Unconditional Law of existing seemed to give Womankind more of an Independent Power.

Verse 7

But the deliberations were Inconclusive because there were Angels who would not disagree with the Person of God; nevertheless, the correspondence within these deliberations produced Doubt and Curious Speculations throughout the Kingdom of Heaven, which mobilized the Energies that had instituted the directional movement of a Negative Existence.

Verse 8

And with deliberations being Inconclusive and our Creator not punishing Satan for making those false Allegations, along with some Angels not disagreeing with Satan's Claim —God's refusal to respond to Satan's Appeal particularly inspired Satan to grow even bolder against God because now Satan thought that manipulating the Truth was a very strategic and ingenious tactic to oust the Person of God from our Creator's Throne.

Verse 9

And so, in Satan's continuous endeavor to defy the Person of God—Satan proceeded forward in trespassing onto the Paradise Garden of Heaven to seduce a Woman into having Unmarital Sex with him, thereby producing the corroborating evidence intended to prove that Humankind will Not Surely Die for violating our Creator's Sacred Rites of Marriage.

Verse 10

And let it be reiterated that it was our Creator's Plan to not immediately punish Satan for his defiance, because not only must our Creator allow the Cause and Effects of Sin to take its course, whereby to Perfect Humankind's creation—but also, if our Creator had punished Satan at the time the Allegations were made, the inquiry of whether our Creator punished Satan due to Satan lying or due to Satan revealing the Truth would still have existed, because Satan is the Accuser, and his defiance is the Cause of Evil.

Section 1: The Psychological Interpretation

Verse 11

Now, to understand the actual incident of Satan trespassing onto the Paradise Garden of Heaven to seduce a Woman, the translation of the Biblical version must be interpreted; and as such:

1. The Paradise Garden of Heaven was interpreted as the Garden of Eden.

2. Satan was interpreted as the Serpent.

3. The Woman seduced by Satan was interpreted as Eve.

4. The First Man created was interpreted as Adam.

5. The Spiritual Conflict between Good and Evil was interpreted as the Tree of Knowledge of Good and Evil.

6. Our Creator's Sacred Rites of Marriage was interpreted as the Tree of Life.

Verse 12

And to comprehend the Psychology at the time of said incident, understand that:

1. Lying on and/or to another person was prohibited—especially lying on and/or to God.

2. Satan was known throughout all of the Kingdoms as God's most reliable Servant.

3. The Paradise Garden of Heaven was kept secured by the First Man created and was where Women who were to become Blessed-In Marriage with the Love of our Creator were taken to be groomed as Wives. But along with not responding to Satan's Appeal, the First Man created also neglected his duties, which allowed Satan to trespass onto the Paradise Garden of Heaven, thereby making a young, innocent Virgin vulnerable and naive to Satan's defiance and seduction as she was introduced to New Experiences that aroused her attention, sensations, and curiosity.

4. The Woman seduced was the young, innocent Virgin who, while in the Paradise Garden of Heaven, was sequestered from having any knowledge of Satan's Appeal to the Angels of Heaven. All she was aware of was that she was going to become Blessed-In Marriage with the Love of our Creator—

but she did not know exactly How or Who she was to be Given-In Marriage to.

Section 2: The Cause of Action Against Our Creator's Universal Laws of Existence

Verse 13

Now, when speaking with the Woman in the Paradise Garden of Heaven, Satan did not blatantly call the Person of God a liar as he had in his Appeal to the Angels of Heaven. Instead, he manipulated the Truth to make the Woman believe that she had misunderstood the process of becoming Blessed-In Marriage with the Love of our Creator.

Verse 14

And in defiance, Satan beguiled the Woman into believing that she would not Surely Die for indulging in sexual relations with him, thereby tricking the Woman into thinking that it was through him that she would become Blessed-In Marriage with the Love of our Creator.

Verse 15

In beguiling the Woman, Satan made three (3) interrogative points of reference:

(1) The first reference asked, "Why would God create an act to be done only to prohibit Humankind from doing the act that He created Humankind to do?" In this, Satan used the parable of God creating a Tree of fruit and then telling Humankind not to eat from

the tree because they would surely die. Satan's point of reference was that if Humankind would Surely Die from eating the fruit, then "Why would God create the Tree of Fruit in the first place?"

(2) The second reference noted that the Woman was placed in the Paradise Garden of Heaven specifically to become Blessed-In Marriage with the Love of our Creator and that he (Satan) was the husband to whom she was to be Given-In Marriage. Satan explained his point of reference as to why he was in the Paradise Garden of Heaven at that time and why the Person of God was not.

(3) The third reference alluded to the selection of a Partner for Marriage, where Womankind actually has the Free Will to have Sex with whomever she chooses because it is her body, which our Creator has made a Crown of Blessing. It is her body that will tell her if and when she is ready to have Sex. Satan's point of reference was that God speaks to us through the activated Energies of Love that are within our creation.

Verse 16

While in actuality, the Truth was that:

1. The Person of God was to bestow our Creator's Spiritual Blessings of Glory upon the Woman's creation.

2. The Person of God was to be the Husband to whom the Woman was to be Given-In Marriage.

3. Any sexual relations or activities not authorized in accordance with our Creator's Universal Laws of Existence and prescribed by the established Authorities of our

Creator's Throne were forbidden, as Humankind would Surely Die for violating our Creator's Sacred Rites of Marriage.

Verse 17

But with the Person of God absent from the Paradise Garden of Heaven, Satan made it seem as though God had placed him (Satan) in the Paradise Garden of Heaven, awaiting her to act in response to the activated Energies of Love that were within her. This allowed Satan to scheme on the Woman's anticipation to engage in the activities of Sex.

Verse 18

Upon sexually approaching and touching the Woman, Satan eventually seduced her into having sexual intercourse with him because she thought the sensations she was feeling were the activated Energies of Love, telling her body that she was ready to have sex and that Satan was the person with whom she was to engage in sexual relations. This was because Satan was arousing her in a way that the Person of God had never made her feel.

Verse 19

When the First Man created arrived at the Paradise Garden of Heaven, the Woman then realized that she had been tricked. In her attempts to undo her mistake, she persuaded the First Man created to redo the marriage ceremony for the Love of our Creator. However, it was the act of Infidelity between Satan and the Woman that initiated the Cause and

Effects of Sin and created the First Cause of Action against our Creator's Universal Laws of Existence.

Section 3: The Indictment Hearing

Verse 20

Due to his negligence in not keeping the Paradise Garden of Heaven secured, the First Man created became just as responsible for the Infidel act committed by Satan and the Woman upon redoing the Marriage Ceremony to Bless-in the Woman as a Crown of Glory in his attempts to undo the Cause and Effects of Sin. As a result, the First Man created was indicted by our Creator's Omnipotent Court of Universal Law and charged with Obstruction of Justice, Negligence, and Incompetence for failing to uphold his obligations and responsibilities as the Crowned King of Heaven.

Verse 21

Due to the fact that the Woman made the choice to believe that God had misinformed her, although she was deceived by Satan, she chose for all of Womankind the position to live in Sin and without the Love of our Creator as the Crowned King of Heaven. As a result, the Woman was indicted by our Creator's Omnipotent Court of Universal Law and charged with Fornication and Conspiracy to undermine the Authority of our Creator's Throne for the Infidel act that gave Satan power over God.

Verse 22

Due to Satan's defiant actions against the Person of God and against our Creator's Universal Laws of Existence, Satan was indicted by our Creator's Omnipotent Court of Universal Law and charged with Trespassing, giving False Testimony, Fornication, Treason, and Conspiracy to undermine the Authority of our Creator's Throne for the Infidel act that created the First Cause of Action against our Creator's Universal Laws of Existence.

Verse 23

Upon being indicted by our Creator's Omnipotent Court of Universal Law, Satan presented the act of Infidelity between him and the Woman as evidence that Humankind would not Surely Die for violating our Creator's Sacred Rites of Marriage. In doing so, he corroborated his Claim and allegations, challenging the Person of God for the Rights to sit upon our Creator's Throne.

Verse 24

Satan argued that the only way a person would Surely Die for violating our Creator's Sacred Rites of Marriage was for the Person of God to kill that person who violated. In doing so, the Person of God would also be violating our Creator's Universal Laws of Existence.

Verse 25

And for the Person of God to violate our Creator's Universal Laws of Existence in order to uphold our Creator's Sacred

Rites of Marriage, such an act would be hypocrisy—thereby proving that:

(1) the Love of our Creator, who is the Person of God, is incompetent as the Crowned King of Heaven,

(2) our Creator's Sacred Rites of Marriage are an unjust abuse of Authority, which imposes restrictions that limit the potentials of other creations, and

(3) Satan's Claim that living in accordance with an Unconditional Law of existing would be "more pleasurable" than living in accordance with our Creator's Universal Laws of Existence does have merit for a Universal Trial Hearing.

Verse 26

And it was duly noted by our Creator's Omnipotent Court of Universal Law that Satan did risk death to seek the Truth of dying for violating our Creator's Sacred Rites of Marriage, in which Satan's definition of to *Surely Die* meant that upon committing an act of Sin, that person will instantaneously be turned into dust and cease to exist.

Verse 27

But God's definition of to *Surely Die* means that upon committing an act of Sin, that person will be banished from the Kingdom of Heaven and deprived of receiving the Spiritual Blessings that maintain an Everlasting Life — whereas, in time, that person will Surely Die of natural causes from not being provided the proper Sustenances needed for our Creator's Spiritual Existence to forever function within the embodiment of their creation.

Verse 28

And in consideration of the facts, our Creator's Omnipotent Court of Universal Law deemed that the act of Infidelity between Satan and the Woman was invalid evidence to corroborate Satan's Claim or allegations against the Person of God—but due to Humankind not having an objective understanding of the Relativity of God, *more time* was needed to show all of Humankind exactly how Humankind will Surely Die for violating our Creator's Sacred Rites of Marriage.

Verse 29

And it was decided that before our Creator's Omnipotent Court of Universal Law can Rule to punish Satan for his defiance, the Court must, by Due Process of Universal Law, establish that Satan's Claim and his allegations against the Person of God are false and that Humankind, in accordance with God's definition, will *in time* Surely Die for violating our Creator's Sacred Rites of Marriage.

Verse 30

And therefore, being that this act of Infidelity between Satan and the Woman had initiated this course of action to settle the Spiritual Conflict between Good and Evil, our Creator's Omnipotent Court of Universal Law had ruled to sentence the Woman and the First Man created to punishment, which subjected all of Humankind to experience the Realities of a Negative Existence under the Rule of Satan for approximately six thousand years.

Verse 31

And thereupon enacting a Motion to Remand Satan onto the Kingdoms of the Earth, our Creator's Omnipotent Court of Universal Law had issued a Universal Decree that closed the Gates of Heaven and ordered everyone who resided within the Kingdoms of Heaven and Earth to thereby undertake the Due process of settling the Spiritual Conflict between Good and Evil.

Section 4: The Universal Decree for the Due Process of Settling the Spiritual Conflict between Good and Evil

Verse 32

Now, to settle the Spiritual Conflict between Good and Evil, our Creator's Omnipotent Court of Universal Law had enacted a Motion to Remand Satan onto the Kingdoms of the Earth, whereby Satan was given an expirational period of Dominion upon the Earth's Living—to thereby institute the undertaking course that will produce the Trial Evidence needed to prove that living in accordance with an Unconditional Law of existing is "More Pleasurable" than living in accordance with our Creator's Universal Laws of Existence.

Verse 33

And with this Motion to Remand Satan onto the Kingdoms of the Earth, a Universal Decree was issued by our Creator's Omnipotent Court of Universal Law, whereby it was so ordered that everyone who resided within the Kingdom of Heaven, including the Person of God, and everyone who resides within the Kingdoms of the Earth must undertake the Due Process of settling the Spiritual Conflict between Good and Evil.

Verse 34

And thereupon issuing this Universal Decree for the Due Process of settling the Spiritual Conflict between Good and Evil, our Creator's Omnipotent Court of Universal Law had closed the Gates of Heaven for the purposes of producing the Objective Understanding needed to show that Humankind will "Surely Die" for violating our Creator's Sacred Rites of Marriage.

Verse 35

Wherein the allotted Time given for Satan to prove his Claim was also incorporated into a Time-Period that will give Humankind the opportunity to assess within their creation the Virtuous Capacity for the activated Energies of Love—to thereby measure each person's Potential of becoming proven Worthy of sitting upon our Creator's Throne.

Verse 36

Whereby it was established by our Creator's Omnipotent Court of Universal Law that from the time of closing the Gates of Heaven until the End-time of Satan's Dominion upon the Earth's living, the established Provisions for settling the Spiritual Conflict between Good and Evil will process the Perfection of Humankind's creation.

Verse 37

And these established Provisions for settling the Spiritual Conflict between Good and Evil will be based upon Humankind's Free Will to either:

• *"continue" living in accordance with an Unconditional Law of existing and "without" the Love of our Creator, or*

• *"begin" living in accordance with our Creator's Universal Laws of Existence and "with" the Love of our Creator as the Crowned King of Heaven.*

Verse 38

And from this Due Process of settling the Spiritual Conflict between Good and Evil, the established Provisions in the action taken to process the Perfection of Humankind's creation will determine the class destinations within our Creator's Universal Existence of One Love through a Universal Trial proceeding that will be known as the Judgment of True Love, in which time our Creator's Omnipotent Court of Universal Law will "evaluate

Humankind's Desire to Need to Live with the Love of our Creator as our Heavenly Father's Crowned King of Heaven."

Section 5: The Realities of a Negative Existence

Verse 39

Now, upon the closing of the Gates of Heaven, Humankind began to produce the Negative Energies of a Universal Desire to Need to Live "without" the Love of our Creator as the Crowned King of Heaven—thereby propelling the physical Properties of our Creator's Universal Existence to operate within the Realities of a Negative Existence.

Verse 40

And although the Creative Energies of our Creator's Desire to Need to Live within the Elements of the Universe generate an Existence of Life for Humankind to live within the Realities of a Negative Existence, Humankind cannot sustain the activated Energies of Love within the embodiment of their creation because the Conductivity to the Negative Energies of a Universal Desire to Need to Live without the Love of our Creator as the Crowned King of Heaven produces "Death."

Verse 41

And by definition, Death is the expiration of Life—because Death cannot occur unless Life is given first.

Verse 42

And the conduct induced from the Negative Energies of a Universal Desire to Need to Live without the Love of our Creator as the Crowned King of Heaven is reflected as being Evil because, by definition, Evil is the induced Negative Energies of a Universal Desire to Need to Live without the Love of our Creator as the Crowned King of Heaven.

Verse 43

And within the Physics of our Creator's Universal Existence, Evil is induced by the Cause and Effects of Sin—because the results from the Cause and Effects of Sin produce Negative Energies.

Verse 44

And by definition, Sin is the violation, offense, and/or erred actions that oppose our Creator's Universal Laws of Existence, whereby:

1. As a Violation, Sin is a deliberate transgression against God's Authority and Order.

2. As an Offense, Sin is the committed infraction of an ethical, moral, or social code.

3. As an Error, Sin is the act, assertion, or belief that deviates from what is correct, right, and/or true.

Verse 45

And it is the Cause and Effect of Sin that propels the Conductivity of Evil, which transmits within the Physics of our Creator's Universal Existence—the Negative Energies of a Universal Desire to Need to Live without the Love of our Creator as the Crowned King of Heaven.

Verse 46

And it is the Conductivity of Evil, which perpetuates the physical Properties of our Creator's Universal Existence to operate within the Realities of a Negative Existence, as Humankind experiences the expirational process of Life—thereby giving meaning to the occurrence of Death.

Verse 47

But for the purpose of establishing an Objective Understanding of the Relativity of God, it is in experiencing Death within the Realities of a Negative Existence that Humankind will have the actual realistic comprehension of:

(1) the Consequences of not obeying and worshipping the Person of God in accordance with our Creator's Universal Laws of Existence, and

(2) the Reality of living without the actual Person of God as the established Authority of our Creator's Spiritual Existence within creation.

Verse 48

And by living within the Realities of a Negative Existence, whereby to receive an Objective Understanding of the Relativity of God—Humankind will be able to perceive the actual process of developing the Perfection of Humankind's creation upon undertaking the course of combat that will settle the Spiritual Conflict between Good and Evil.

Section 6: Our Creator's Divine Covenant with Humankind

Verse 49

Now, upon issuing the Universal Decree for the Due Process of settling the Spiritual Conflict between Good and Evil, our Creator knew that, "in time," Humankind would experience Death within the Realities of a Negative Existence because, after closing the Gates of Heaven, the Kingdoms of the Earth had become electromagnetically disconnected from the Circuitry that illuminates our Creator's Light, whereby Humankind was unable to receive the Sustenance needed to maintain an Everlasting Life.

Verse 50

But specifically upon the Death of the First Man created, who was the Person of God—the established Authority of our Creator's Spiritual Existence was no longer embodied within Humankind's creation, thereby leaving Humankind to produce the Negative Energies that perpetuate the Realities of a Negative Existence.

Verse 51

And by living within the Realities of a Negative Existence without the established Authority of our Creator's Spiritual

Existence embodied within Humankind's creation—Humankind was deprived of the authoritative direction needed to overcome the Imperfections of their creation for their Resurrection back to the Realities of a Positive Existence, whereby Humankind was subjected to the Atrocities and Afflictions of Evil due to the Kingdoms of the Earth being under the Dominion of Satan.

Verse 52

Wherefore, upon issuing the Universal Decree for the Due Process of settling the Spiritual Conflict between Good and Evil, our Creator established a Divine Covenant with Humankind, which promised all of Humankind that, upon the fulfillment of our Creator's Chosen People undergoing the suffering Tribulations of upholding the Conditional Principles of our Creator's Spiritual Existence—our Creator would reopen the Gates of Heaven and unite the Kingdom of Heaven with the Kingdoms of the Earth.

Verse 53

Because, by definition, the Conditional Principles of our Creator's Spiritual Existence are the Righteous Mode and Moral Standards that will maintain the Conductivity that produces the Positive Energies of a Universal Desire to Need to Live with the Love of our Creator as the Crowned King of Heaven.

Verse 54

And by suffering the Tribulations of upholding the Conditional Principles of our Creator's Spiritual Existence, our Creator's Chosen People will establish the Provisions and Proportions needed to Standardize the Measures for living in accordance with our Creator's Universal Laws of Existence—whereby our Creator, from the blood lineage of our Creator's Chosen People, will be able to (re)create the embodied creation of our Creator's Spiritual Existence as the reincarnated Person of God, who will establish the Direction and Disposition that will lead Humankind in the Universal Resurrection to a Positive Existence.

Verse 55

And with this Divine Covenant, our Creator established that, for the Due Process of settling the Spiritual Conflict between Good and Evil, the reincarnated Person of God would be borne of our Creator's Chosen People in the appointed End-time of Satan's Dominion upon the Earth's living, to thereby execute the Judicial proceedings for the Confrontation of Truth; in which time will our Creator's Omnipotent Court of Universal Law establish the Venue and Jurisdictions for the Judgment of True Love through a "Motion to Suppress" Satan's Allegations that God makes restrictions that limit the Potentials of other creations.

Section 7: Satan's Burden of Proof

Verse 56

Now, for the Due Process of settling the Spiritual Conflict between Good and Evil, Satan was given approximately (6) six thousand years of Dominion upon the Earth's living, to thereby create for Humankind's experience a living in accordance with an Unconditional Law of existing.

Verse 57

And with this (6) six thousand years of Dominion upon the Earth's living, Satan carries the Burden of producing the Trial Evidence needed to prove that living in accordance with an Unconditional Law of existing is "More Pleasurable" than living in accordance with our Creator's Universal Laws of Existence.

Verse 58

But in order to produce this Trial Evidence, Satan must demonstrate the Forces of Evil that exist within the nature of Humankind's creation as being stronger than the Spiritual Forces of Good deriving from within our Creator's Throne, thereby discrediting our Creator's Divine Covenant with Humankind.

Verse 59

Because, as pre-determined by our Creator's Omnipotent Court of Universal Law, if living in accordance with an Unconditional Law of existing is "More Pleasurable" than living in accordance with our Creator's Universal Laws of Existence, then, while living within the Realities of a Negative Existence, the Forces of Evil that exist within the nature of Humankind's creation should be able to prevent the Spiritual Forces of Good deriving from within our Creator's Throne from establishing the Direction and Disposition needed to lead Humankind in the Universal Resurrection to a Positive Existence.

Verse 60

Wherefore, in producing the Trial Evidence needed to prove that living in accordance with an Unconditional Law of existing is "More Pleasurable" than living in accordance with our Creator's Universal Laws of Existence, Satan was permitted to establish the Battlefields of a Negatively Induced Environment within the Kingdoms of the Earth, thereby processing the Undertaking Combat between the Spiritual Forces of Good and the Forces of Evil.

Verse 61

Because, by Due Process of Universal Law, in order to settle the Spiritual Conflict between Good and Evil, the attested Conquest from the Undertaking Combat within the Battlefields of a Negatively Induced Environment must be reflected through the Will-Power of Humankind's nature.

Verse 62

Which means that in settling the Spiritual Conflict between Good and Evil, either:

(A) *The Spiritual Forces of Good must reflect within Humankind's nature the Will-Power to observe our Creator's Universal Laws of Existence,*

or

(B) *The Forces of Evil must reflect within Humankind's nature the Will-Power to observe an Unconditional Law of existing.*

Verse 63

And due to the fact that Satan carries the Burden of producing the Trial Evidence needed to prove that living in accordance with an Unconditional Law of existing is "More Pleasurable" than living in accordance with our Creator's Universal Laws of Existence, for the purposes of settling the Spiritual Conflict between Good and Evil, Satan must prevent the Spiritual Forces of Good from accumulating the Divine Will-Power to institute the Stabilizing Measures for balancing the Equilibrium of living within our Creator's Universal Existence of One Love.

CHAPTER FIVE: THE UNDERTAKING COMBAT WITHIN THE BATTLEFIELDS OF A NEGATIVELY INDUCED ENVIRONMENT

Verse 1

Now for the Due Process of settling the Spiritual Conflict between Good and Evil, Satan was given (6) six-thousand years of dominion upon the Earth's living – to thereby produce the Trial Evidence needed to prove his Claim that living in accordance with an Unconditional Law of existing is "more pleasurable" than living in accordance with our Creator's Universal Laws of Existence.

Verse 2

And to produce this Trial Evidence needed to prove said Claim, it was ordered by our Creator's Omnipotent Court of Universal Law that Satan must "prevent the embodied (re) creation of our Creator's Spiritual Existence borne of our Creator's Chosen People from establishing the Direction and Disposition that will lead Humankind in the Universal

Resurrection to living within the Realities of a Positive Existence" – whereby to discredit our Creator's Divine Covenant with Humankind.

Verse 3

And to prevent the embodied (re) creation of our Creator's Spiritual Existence borne of our Creator's Chosen People from establishing the Direction and Disposition that will lead Humankind in the Universal Resurrection to living within the Realities of a Positive Existence, Satan was allowed to establish within the Kingdoms of the Earth – the Battlefields of a negatively induced environment.

Verse 4

And by definition, the Battlefields of a negatively induced environment are the structuralized spheres and schemes of Evil Conductivity, in which it is designed to systematically infect an Evil Will upon Humankind's cultural growth and development – whereby to make the people Stand for the Wrongs of an Evil Existence and content with living in accordance with an Unconditional Law of existing.

Verse 5

But to establish the Battlefields of a negatively induced environment within the Kingdoms of the Earth, the Spheres and Schemes of Evil Conductivity must be structuralized to preserve the cultivation of Humankind's Free-Will relations.

Verse 6

Because by structuralizing the Spheres and Schemes of Evil Conductivity to preserve the cultivation of Humankind's Free-Will relations, the undertaking combat within the Battlefields of a negatively induced environment will be processed to reflect through Humankind's nature – the Will-Power that will demonstrate whether or not the Forces of Evil that exist within the nature of Humankind's creation are stronger than the Spiritual Forces of Good deriving from within our Creator's Throne, whereby to ascertain the Trial Evidence needed to prove if living in accordance with an Unconditional Law of existing is "more pleasurable" than living in accordance with our Creator's Universal Laws of Existence.

Verse 7

And in structuralizing the Spheres and Schemes of Evil Conductivity within the Kingdoms of the Earth, whereby to preserve the cultivation of Humankind's Free-Will relations – it was designed so that:

(1) The Educational Spheres will be incorporated to institute an Accreditation System that will promote the manipulations of living in accordance with an Unconditional Law of existing – wherein to execute the evil schemes that will teach Immoral Values and indoctrinate Deviant Principles.

(2) The Economical Spheres will be incorporated to regulate

a Monetary System that will promote the Livelihood of living without the Person of God as our Heavenly Father's

Crowned King of Heaven – wherein to execute the evil schemes that will control the Distribution of Wealth and classify the Privileges of Capitalism, and

(3) The Political Spheres will be incorporated to enforce a democracy system that will promote the Reigns of Satan's dominion upon the Earth's living – wherein to execute the evil schemes that will legislate the Campaigns of Sin and assert the Prejudices of Conquest, and

(4) The Social Spheres will be incorporated to produce an entertainment system that will promote the Seduction of a Universal Desire to Need to Live – wherein to execute the evil schemes that will influence Vain Conduct and glorify the Rewards of Idolatry.

Verse 8

And upon the structuralization of the Spheres and Schemes of Evil Conductivity within the Kingdoms of the Earth, the accumulated Forces will be able to induce the Evil that exists within the nature of Humankind's creation – whereby to continuously propel the Negative Energies of a Universal Desire to Need to Live without the Love of our Creator as the Crowned King of Heaven, wherein to reflect within Humankind's nature, the Will-Power to observe an Unconditional Law of existing.

Section 1: Humankind's Exodus from the Kingdom of Heaven

Verse 9

Now after remanding Satan to the Kingdoms of the Earth, our Creator's Omnipotent Court of Universal Law had ordered everyone who resided within the Kingdom of Heaven to begin cultivating their own Kingdoms upon the Earth – in which time every person within the Kingdom of Heaven was given the Free-Will to either:

(1) follow Satan in his endeavors to prove that living in accordance with an Unconditional Law of existing is "More Pleasurable" than living in accordance with our Creator's Universal Laws of Existence,

-or-

(2) follow their own aspirations in becoming proven worthy of sitting upon our Creator's Throne,

-or-

(3) continue worshipping and obeying the First Man created in accordance with our Creator's Universal Laws of Existence.

Verse 10

But despite the First Man created being relieved of sitting upon our Creator's Throne as the Crowned King of Heaven, he still remained the embodied creation and established Authority of our Creator's Spiritual Existence – and as "the embodied creation of our Creator's Spiritual Existence," the First Man created was preserved with (4) four thousand years of immortality; which was recorded as the time Before Christ (B.C).

Verse 11

And with the Gates of Heaven being closed, the First Man created as the established Authority of our Creator's Spiritual Existence had allowed our Creator to centralize and communalize the Spiritual Realms of Heaven – to thereby process Humankind's productive cultivation within the Kingdoms of the Earth.

Verse 12

And by definition, the Spiritual Realms of Heaven are the controlled preservations of the Electromagnetic Field that generates and directs the Positive Energies of a Universal Desire to Need to Live with the Love of our Creator.

Verse 13

And from the Spiritual Realms of Heaven, our Creator performed Miracles and gave the People of the Earth – visions and prophecies that infected a Moral Will upon Humankind's cultural growth and development, in contrast to the Evil Will that was systematically infected through the Battlefields of a Negatively Induced Environment.

Verse 14

And so, as Humankind's actual Exodus from the Kingdom of Heaven began:

(1) those people who chose to follow Satan were cast out of the Kingdom of Heaven and traveled the Northern Hemisphere of the Earth to create the genes of people who were originally cultivated to live in accordance with an Unconditional Law of existing; and this cultivation of people inhabited what is now known as the Kingdom of Europe,

(2) those people who chose to follow their own aspirations traveled the Western Hemisphere of the Earth to cultivate a living in accordance with the Laws of Nature; and this indigenous people inhabited what is now known as the Kingdom of America, and

(3) those people who chose to continue worshipping and obeying the First Man created traveled the Southern Hemisphere of the Earth to establish the genes of our Creator's Chosen People; who inhabited what is now known as the Kingdom of Africa.

Verse 15

But in processing Humankind's cultivation within the Kingdoms of the Earth while preserving Humankind's Free-Will relations, those of our Creator's Chosen People who later in time were ostracized for violating our Creator's Universal Laws of Existence, along with those people within the Northern and Western Hemisphere of the Earth who later in time chose to re-establish a positive relationship with our Creator – they all traveled to the Eastern Hemisphere of the Earth to formulate the different Nationalities of the World; and those people inhabited what is now known as the Kingdom of Asia.

Verse 16

And although Satan was given dominion over the Earth's living for (6) six thousand years, in the time Before Christ (B.C) while the Kingdoms of the Earth were being cultivated – our Creator's Chosen People's African Kingdom dwelled within the Spiritual Realms of Heaven and were protected from the Conductivity of Evil, due to the First Man created continued existence as the established Authority of our Creator's Spiritual Existence within Humankind's creation; in whom the people continued to worship and obey in accordance with our Creator's Universal Laws of Existence.

Verse 17

And because the established Authority of our Creator's Spiritual Existence continued to exist within Humankind's creation, those people who came to formulate the different nationalities of the World – in their combat against the Forces of Evil within the Battlefields of a Negatively Induced Environment, they were given Messianic Visions and Prophecies in which directed them in the undertaking course that would lead their descendants back to the Kingdom of Heaven.

Verse 18

But also during the time Before Christ (B.C), as the Forces of Evil within the Battlefields of a negativity induced environment were combating the different nationalities of the World, in preparation for when Death would come upon the First Man created – Satan was formulating the Powers of Evil, to thereby create an Empire that would mislead all of Humankind into becoming consensual with living in accordance with an Unconditional Law of existing.

Verse 19

And it was thereupon the death of the First Man created that the Powers of Evil conceived the birth of Jesus Christ, who had falsely enacted the fulfillment of the Messianic Prophecies that were given to the different nationalities of the World – upon which Satan, in his last (2) two thousand years of dominion upon the Earth's living, created the Religious Empire of Christianity.

Verse 20

And it is the last (2) two thousand years of dominion upon the Earth's living that is the time after the death of the First Man created, which became defined by the Powers of Evil as the Anno-Dominion (A.D) – whereby dating the years of Satan's Rule within the Kingdoms of the Earth without the established authority of our Creator's Spiritual Existence within Humankind's creation.

Verse 21

And in those years of Satan's Rule within the Kingdoms of the Earth without the established authority of our Creator's Spiritual Existence within Humankind's creation, it was our Creator's Chosen People who inherited the obligations of combating against the Forces of Evil within the Battlefields of a Negatively Induced Environment (on behalf of the Spiritual Forces of Good) – and this undertaking combat to overcome the Forces of Evil within the Battlefields of a Negatively Induced Environment became the Struggles of Survival for our Creator's Chosen People.

Section 2: In the Beginning Times of Our Creator's Chosen People's African Kingdom

Verse 22

Now, in the Beginning times of Humankind's Exodus from out the Kingdom of Heaven, our Creator's Chosen People lived in peace and harmony within the tribal communities as a Kingdom united within the Spiritual Realms of Heaven.

Verse 23

And our Creator's Chosen People's African Kingdom was united because the Land and the People were governed by our Creator, who lived within creation as the King, and this creation of our Creator is the Person of God who was the First Man created—who gave Life to Humankind.

Verse 24

And as the King, our Creator governed the Land and the People with "Strictness" because that was the only way to maintain order and protect the Kingdom from the Evil that exists within the nature of Humankind's creation.

Verse 25

And by definition, the Evil that exists within the nature of Humankind's creation is the negative inclination that comes from the Pride that each person has of themselves.

Verse 26

And although it is good to have Pride in oneself, the negative inclination of too much Pride in oneself creates Vanity—and Vanity promotes Greed and Selfishness, which subsequently results in the growth of Jealousy, which in turn fuels Hatred.

Verse 27

But in our Creator's Chosen People's African Kingdom, the King kept the Evil that exists within the nature of Humankind's creation in check—as it was a King's Rule that those people who challenged the King's authority and/or violated our Creator's Universal Laws of Existence were to be "Ostracized" from our Creator's Chosen People's African Kingdom.

Verse 28

And of course, eventually, there were people who did go astray and violated our Creator's Universal Laws of Existence—and those people were ostracized from our Creator's Chosen People's African Kingdom.

Verse 29

But mind you, those people who were ostracized from the Kingdom—they were greatly loved by family members and by many people in the Kingdom.

Verse 30

And although everybody was given a choice to either stay within the Kingdom or leave with those people being ostracized, (in which many chose to stay within the Kingdom) nevertheless, the ostracism of family members and loved ones left the people with Bitterness towards the King's governing Strictness.

Verse 31

And this Bitterness soon energized the questioning of "whether or not the King's governing Strictness was right," because many of our ancestors thought that the King's Rule to ostracize was too harsh—as many felt that instead of ostracizing them, the King could have forgiven them and given them another chance; and this further ignited discussions of living in accordance with an Unconditional Law of existing.

Verse 32

And then there were Tribal leaders who accused the King of not loving the people within the Kingdom and having Vanity within the nature of his creation, which ultimately did not allow the King to admit that his governing Strictness was wrong and too harsh.

Verse 33

But the King's Rule to ostracize was our Creator taking the position of—"This is my house and if you do not obey and abide by my Laws and Authority, then you must leave my house and go build your own house."

Verse 34

And also, our Creator, who is all-knowing, knew and understood beforehand that the questioning and bitterness that His People had towards the King's governing Strictness was the result of the People not having an Objective Understanding of the Relativity of God.

Verse 35

And by definition, the Relativity of God is simply Humankind's comprehension of the value and significance that the Person of God has in connection with Humankind's existence and well-being.

Verse 36

And without an objective understanding of the Relativity of God, Humankind could never become Perfected—because the People will not have an actual realistic comprehension of the Reality of living without the Person of God as the established Authority of our Creator's Spiritual Existence.

Verse 37

And it was understood by our Creator that in order to perfect Humankind, our Creator was going to have to allow Humankind to experience living "without" the Person of God as the established Authority of our Creator's Spiritual Existence—to thereby show Humankind the value and significance of the King's governing Strictness; which meant that, in time, our Creator was going to have to permit the Death of the First Man created.

Verse 38

But in the time before the Death of the First Man created, our Creator used the method of Ostracism to produce other civilizations and Nationalities for the purposes of establishing the Battlefields of a negatively induced environment.

Verse 39

Because those people who got ostracized from our Creator's Chosen People's African Kingdom, in time, began to develop a Hatred towards the King and our Creator's Chosen People's African Kingdom—thereby establishing a relationship with our Creator that was "different" from the relationship our Creator's Chosen People had with our Creator.

Verse 40

And established by those people ostracized from our Creator's Chosen People's African Kingdom was a Negative relationship that gave meaning to a Desire to Need to Live "without" the Love of our Creator, in which gave each person the Free-Will to either:

• follow Satan in his Endeavors to prove that living in accordance with an Unconditional Law of existing is "More Pleasurable" than living in accordance with our Creator's Universal Laws of Existence, or

• follow their own Aspirations in becoming proven Worthy of sitting upon our Creator's Throne.

Verse 41

And conceived from this negative relationship was the Knowledge of Evil, which is defined as the study, observation, and application to the induced Negative Energies of a Desire to Need to Live without the Love of our Creator as the established Authority of our Creator's Spiritual Existence.

Verse 42

But to establish the Battlefields of a Negatively Induced Environment upon producing other civilizations and Nationalities, our Creator had allowed a certain people to develop a "Strategic Method" that uses the Knowledge of Evil to manipulate the Truth and control the Land – and these certain people with this Strategic Method had come to be the Powers of Evil.

Section 3: The Powers of Evil within the Battlefields of a Negatively Induced Environment

Verse 43

Now in the time Before Christ (B.C.), as our Creator used the method of Ostracism to produce other civilizations and Nationalities – the people who were ostracized from our Creator's Chosen People's African Kingdom were given the Free-Will to either:

• follow Satan in his Endeavors to prove that living in accordance with an Unconditional Law of existing is "More Pleasurable" than living in accordance with our Creator's Universal Laws of Existence, or

• follow their own Aspirations in becoming proven Worthy of sitting upon our Creator's Throne.

Verse 44

And as determined by their Potentials, some of those people who chose to follow Satan in his Endeavors came to be either:

• a Force of Evil – who are directors and motivators to the Spheres and Schemes of Evil Conductivity within the Kingdoms of the Earth, or

• a Power of Evil – who are producers and engineers to the Evil Stratagems that mobilize and regulate the Evil Conductivity within the Battlefields of a negatively induced environment.

Verse 45

And those people who chose to follow their own Aspirations – many came to formulate the different Cultures and Nationalities of the World, who in time comprised the Religious Denominations that were designed to re-establish a Positive relationship with our Creator.

Verse 46

And from these Religious Denominations, each Nationality was given Messianic Visions and Prophecies that directed them in the undertaking course that will lead the descendants of their Nationality back to the Kingdom of Heaven.

Verse 47

And as the Powers of Evil proceeded in establishing the Battlefields of a negatively induced environment within the Kingdoms of the Earth, this undertaking course that will lead each Nationality back to the Kingdom of Heaven – became the Cultural Trials and Tribulations of validating the Conditional Realities of our Creator's Spiritual Existence within their creation; in which time did the Powers of Evil infiltrate the Hebrew Nationality, thus manipulating the True Identity of our Creator's Chosen People.

Verse 48

Because upon being Delivered from bondage by the hands of our Creator, as an agreement to validate the Conditional Realities of our Creator's Spiritual Existence within their creation – it was the Hebrew Nationality who were given our Creator's (10) Ten Commandments and assigned to protect the prophecy of the Messiah fulfilling our Creator's Divine Covenant with Humankind.

Verse 49

Meaning that to validate the Conditional Realities of our Creator's Spiritual Existence within their creation, the Hebrew Nationality is responsible for defending the accuracy of the proclaimed Messiah fulfilling our Creator's Divine Covenant with Humankind by comparison of Keeping our Creator's (10) Ten Commandments.

Verse 50

And in order to protect the prophecy of the Messiah fulfilling our Creator's Divine Covenant with Humankind, the Hebrew Nationality must sustain the Righteous Mode and Moral Provisions that will verify the Judicial Qualifications and Jurisdictions needed to righteously execute Universal Justice.

Verse 51

And by infiltrating the Hebrew Nationality to manipulate the True Identity of our Creator's Chosen People, the Powers of Evil were able to intentionally misinterpret the translation of the Messianic Visions and Prophecies that were given – thereby portraying the Hebrew Nationality as the ancestry of the prophesied Messiah, and depicting the Jewish People, who became tribal descendants of the Hebrew Nationality, as our Creator's Chosen People of God.

Verse 52

And with this misinterpretation of the Jewish people being our Creator's Chosen People of God, the Powers of Evil, upon the Death of the First Man created, were able to conceive the Birth of Jesus Christ, in whom they falsely enacted the fulfillment of our Creator's Divine Covenant with Humankind.

Verse 53

And let it be clarified that in protecting the prophecy of the Messiah fulfilling our Creator's Divine Covenant with Humankind, it was the Hebrew Nationality who rejected Jesus Christ as the prophesied Messiah – because Jesus Christ did not substantiate the Judicial Qualifications and Jurisdictions needed to righteously execute Universal Justice.

Verse 54

And although this rejection led to the crucifixion of Jesus Christ, it also allowed the Powers of Evil to falsely enact the fulfillment of our Creator's Divine Covenant with Humankind by misleading the People to believe that:

(1) Jesus Christ, in being crucified as the "Begotten Son of

God," was the Divine Sacrifice that redeems Humankind of their Sins, and

(2) Upon being crucified on the Cross, Jesus Christ ascended into Heaven to sit upon our Creator's Throne as our Heavenly Father's Crowned King of Heaven, and

(3) By professing Jesus Christ to be the Messiah and Savior, Humankind will be forgiven for their Sins and granted entrance to live in the Kingdom of Heaven.

Verse 55

But to believe that the crucifixion of Jesus Christ redeemed Humankind of their Sins "misleads" Humankind into believing that God has Unconditional Love for Humankind.

Verse 56

And to believe that the actual Person of God has died on Earth and ascended into Heaven to sit upon our Creator's Throne as the Crowned King of Heaven "misleads" Humankind into believing that our Creator's Throne is currently occupied and that our Heavenly Father's Crowned King is governing Humankind's living upon the Earth.

Verse 57

And to believe that Humankind will be granted entrance into the Kingdom of Heaven upon professing Jesus Christ to be the Messiah and Savior "misleads" Humankind into believing that no matter how many times a person Sins or transgresses against our Creator's (10) Ten Commandments or Universal Laws of Existence – their Sins and/or Transgressions will be forgiven without Consequence.

Verse 58

And with the belief of Jesus Christ being the prophesied Messiah and Crowned King of Heaven, the Powers of Evil were able to create the Religious Empire of Christianity – thereby "misleading" Humankind into becoming consensual with living in accordance with an Unconditional Law of existing.

Verse 59

And by definition, living in accordance with an Unconditional Law of existing means that there should be No Requirements or Obligations needed to fulfill the performance, completion, or existence of what is committed or established in the name of Love – which basically means that a person's Desire to Need to Live with another person should not be dependent upon any Conditions.

Verse 60

And by living in accordance with an Unconditional Law of existing, Christianity teaches that:

(1) If a person's Love for another has been committed or established by Partnership and Loyalty, such as the Love a Wife or Husband has for their Spouse – then their Desire to Need to Live with one another should be forever bound by the Understandings and Respect of their Commitment.

(2) If a person's Love for another has been established by Birth and Life, such as the Love a Mother or Father has for their Child -or- the Love a Child has for their Parents – then their Desire to Need to Live with one another should be forever bound by the Wisdom and Honor of their

Family, and

(3) If a person's Love for another has been established by Kinship and Love, such as the Love a Brother or Sister has for their Sibling – then their Desire to Need to Live with one another should be forever bound by the Knowledge and Values of their Ancestry.

Verse 61

And as a Concept of living in accordance with an Unconditional Law of existing, if a person commits an Act of Sin or violates a Law or Commandment – whatever Wrong that was committed can be excused without Consequence upon the Appeal for forgiveness, because it is the Teachings of Christianity that Forgiveness is the greatest expression of a person's Desire to Need to Live with another person.

Verse 62

And so, with the Religious Empire of Christianity, the Powers of Evil were able to mobilize the Forces of Evil within the Battlefields of a Negatively Induced Environment, thereby inducing the Evil that exists within the nature of Humankind's creation to continuously engage in the Conductivity of Evil.

Verse 63

Now in the time Before Christ (B.C.), as the Battlefields of a Negatively Induced Environment were being established within the Kingdoms of the Earth that were "outside" of the Spiritual Realms of Heaven – the evil that exists within the nature of Humankind's creation was also intensifying within our Creator's Chosen People's African Kingdom, wherein the bitterness towards the King's governing strictness eventually brought death upon the First Man created at the end of his (4) four thousand years of Immortality, just as ordained by our Creator.

Verse 64

And in the time After the Death of the First Man created (A.D.), as the Powers of Evil within the Battlefields of a Negatively Induced Environment grew in strength and ability with the Religious Empire of Christianity – Satan proceeded in deceiving the people living within the Northern Hemisphere of the Earth into invading the Kingdom of Africa, to thereby attack the Moralities of our Creator's Chosen People.

Verse 65

Because, for the Due Process of settling the Spiritual Conflict between Good and Evil, Satan must discredit our Creator's Divine Covenant with Humankind – to thereby produce the Trial Evidence needed to prove that living in accordance with an Unconditional Law of existing is "more pleasurable" than living in accordance with our Creator's Universal Laws of Existing.

Verse 66

And to discredit our Creator's Divine Covenant with Humankind, the Powers of Evil must prevent the embodied (re)creation of our Creator's Spiritual Existence, borne of our Creator's Chosen People, from establishing the Direction and Disposition that will lead Humankind in the Universal Resurrection to a Positive Existence.

Verse 67

And so the Undertaking Objective for the Powers of Evil within the Battlefields of a negatively induced environment is to demonstrate the Forces of Evil that exist within the nature of Humankind's creation as being stronger than the Spiritual Forces of Good deriving from within our Creator's Throne.

Verse 68

And to demonstrate the Forces of Evil that exist within the nature of Humankind's creation as being stronger than the Spiritual Forces of Good deriving from within our Creator's Throne, Satan's stratagem was to attack the Moralities of our Creator's Chosen People.

Verse 69

And by attacking the Moralities of our Creator's Chosen People, the Forces of Evil within the Battlefields of a negatively induced environment intended to portray and guide our Creator's Chosen People in demoralizing the Qualities and Standards that exemplify the conduct of living in accordance with our Creator's Universal Laws of Existence – thereby deterring our Creator's Chosen People from upholding the Conditional Principles of our Creator's Spiritual Existence.

Verse 70

Because, in combating against the Forces of Evil within the Battlefields of a negatively induced environment, the undertaking objective for our Creator's Chosen People is for them to sustain the Righteous Qualities and Moral Standards that will maintain the conductivity that produces the Positive energies of a Universal Desire to Need to Live with the Love of our Creator as the Crowned King of Heaven – to thereby enable our Creator to (re)create the embodied creation of our Creator's Spiritual Existence within Humankind's creation, in whom will fulfill our Creator's Divine Covenant with Humankind.

Verse 71

And by upholding the Conditional Principles of our Creator's Spiritual Existence, our Creator's Chosen People will not only establish the Qualities of living within the Standards that exemplify the conduct of living in accordance with our Creator's Universal Laws of Existence – but also, they will protect their Status as the Chosen People of God in whose Heritage is to occupy the Kingdom of Heaven.

Verse 72

And so because the Spiritual Essence within our Creator's Chosen People are genetically the strongest of Humankind, by attacking the Moralities of our Creator's Chosen People – this Satanic stratagem will measure the Will-Power that ascertains the Trial Evidence needed to prove Satan's Claim that living in accordance with an Unconditional Law of existing is "more pleasurable" than living in accordance with our Creator's Universal Laws of Existence.

Verse 73

Which means that in settling the Spiritual Conflict between Good and Evil, either our Creator's Chosen People were going to be Faithful to their Heritage and fulfill the obligations and duties that will allow the Spiritual Forces of Good to reach their Greatest Potential - or - they were going to abandon their African Struggle and permit the Powers of Evil to discredit our Creator's Divine Covenant with Humankind.

Verse 74

Wherefore, it was in initiating the attack on the Moralities of our Creator's Chosen People, did the Powers of Evil with the Religious Empire of Christianity misled people into believing that the Jewish/Hebrew nationality are the Chosen People of God and that the prophesied Messiah is not of African descent, thereby enabling the Forces of Evil to influence the people within the Kingdom of Europe into invading our Creator's Chosen People's African Kingdom.

Verse 75

And therefrom this European invasion of Africa:

• our Creator's Chosen People were killed, kidnapped, raped, enslaved, brainwashed, and persecuted,

• our Creator's Chosen People's African Kingdom was destroyed and dissipated, and

• our Creator's Chosen People's Heritage and Identity were stolen and concealed.

Verse 76

But it was thereupon the European invasion of Africa that our Creator's Chosen People began undergoing the suffering Tribulations of upholding the Conditional Principles of our Creator's Spiritual Existence – to thereby combat against the Forces of Evil within the Battlefields of a Negatively Induced Environment.

Verse 77

And it is the Undertaking Combat within the Battlefields of a Negatively Induced Environment that concludes the Ending process that perceives the development of Humankind's creation.

CHAPTER SIX: ACCEPTING THE REALITIES OF TRUTH

The Absolute, in which is the Completing process that perfects the development of Humankind's creation, begins with Accepting the Realities of Truth.

Verse 1

Now, it was preordained by our Creator's Omnipotent Court of Universal Law that upon the Judicial proceedings for the Confrontation of Truth, Humankind's Free-Will decision to either "continue" living in accordance with an Unconditional Law of existing -or- "begin" living in accordance with our Creator's Universal Laws of Existence – will be based upon each person's acceptance of the Realities of Truth.

Verse 2

And by definition, the Realities of Truth are the harsh facts obtained by our Creator's Chosen People upon combating the Forces of Evil within the Battlefields of a Negatively Induced Environment.

Verse 3

Because, as a result of fulfilling the Undertaking Objective of upholding the Conditional Principles of our Creator's Spiritual Existence, the suffering Tribulations undergone by our Creator's Chosen People will establish the Realities of Truth as the prima facie evidence needed to settle the Spiritual Conflict between Good and Evil.

Verse 4

Whence, at the appointed End-time of Satan's Dominion upon the Earth's living, our Creator's Omnipotent Court of Universal Law will execute the Judicial proceedings for the Confrontation of Truth – in which time will Humankind, by Free-Will, choose to take the "Legal Stance" to either display their "Desire to Need to Live" with -or- without the Love of our Creator as our Heavenly Father's Crowned King of Heaven.

Verse 5

And it is in taking the Legal Stance that will display their "Desire to Need to Live" with the Love of our Creator as our Heavenly Father's Crowned King of Heaven, must Humankind accept the Realities of Truth – to thereby "begin" living in accordance with our Creator's Universal Laws of Existence.

Verse 6

And in order to accept the Realities of Truth for the Due Process of settling the Spiritual Conflict between Good and Evil, Humankind must acknowledge these (4) four harsh facts to be true:

• Harsh Fact One: the African slave descendants called Niggas are our Creator's Chosen People,

• Harsh Fact Two: the blasphemy of Jesus Christ is the Manipulation of the Truth that disguises Satan as God,

• Harsh Fact Three: Satan's Stratagem within the Spiritual Conflict between Good and Evil was to attack the Moralities of our Creator's Chosen People, and

• Harsh Fact Four: the Moralities of our Creator's Chosen People were defended by the Gangster Disciples standardizing the Measures for living in accordance with our Creator's Universal Laws of Existence.

And so, let us review these harsh facts obtained by our Creator's Chosen People upon combating the Forces of Evil within the Battlefields of a Negatively Induced Environment.

Harsh Fact One: The African Slave Descendants called Niggas are our Creator's Chosen People.

Verse 7

Now, within the world's popular religious textbooks, our Creator's Chosen People have been described as the people who are hated by all nations and persecuted for our Heavenly Father's name's sake. (Matthew 10:22 and 24:9, Luke 21:12-19)

Verse 8

This means that our Creator's Chosen People have the same name as our Heavenly Father and that they are hated and Persecuted because they are the people chosen to inherit the Rights to occupy the Kingdom of Heaven.

Verse 9

By definition, to be Hated by all nations because of "name's sake" means that all nations of government and its people will display and have feelings of animosity and malice towards a specific people who are called by a certain name.

Verse 10

Those specific people who are Hated will not receive any assistance in the redevelopment of their own nation from any other nation or government. Instead, those people called by their certain name will be despised and become the objects of offensive and prejudicial behavior solely for the reasons of ancestry.

Verse 11

Not only will they be Hated by other nations of people, but many will display feelings of detestation towards who they are as a people because, when called by their certain name, they become offended due to the discrimination and racism caused by their oppressors.

Verse 12

By definition, to be Persecuted because of "name's sake" means that the people who are called by a certain name will be oppressed and harassed with ill-treatment due to their ancestral bloodline and heritage.

Verse 13

Those specific people Persecuted because of name's sake will be physically subjugated by unjust and tyrannical use of force and authority, as well as being victims of mental and spiritual depression.

Verse 14

While living under the Rule of an unjust and tyrannical nation, the sufferings and tribulations of those people Persecuted because of name's sake will not be conceded or given proper compensation from their oppressor.

Verse 15

Just as prophesied within the world's popular religious textbooks, our Creator's Chosen People will suffer in bondage to a wicked nation for over 400 years, and only by the hand of our Creator will our Creator's Chosen People be delivered from their oppressor. (Genesis 15:13)

Verse 16

This means that up until the end-time of Satan's (6) six thousand years of dominion upon the Earth's living, our Creator's Chosen People, who are the people Hated by all nations and Persecuted because of our Heavenly Father's name's sake, will "continue" to be enslaved and discriminated against by the unjust and tyrannical nation.

Verse 17

In recognizing the Truth of our existing realities, the African slave descendants called Niggas are the people who have suffered in bondage for over 400 years and are the people who continue to be enslaved and discriminated against by the unjust and tyrannical Nation of America – specifically in the United States of America.

Verse 18

Proof of the fact that Niggas are the people Hated by all nations and Persecuted because of name's sake is displayed by the relations of the many different nations of people living within the United States of America. The United States of America represents the melting pot of the world, where immigrants of different nations and cultures form an integrated society.

Verse 19

But to confuse the Reality of Fact that the African slave descendants called Niggas are our Creator's Chosen People, the Powers of Evil within the Battlefields of a negatively induced environment have manipulated the True Identity of our Creator's Chosen People by establishing the Misconceptions and Ills of our Creator's Chosen People's African "Name."

Verse 20

Because in its actualities:

(1) The Misconceptions of our Creator's Chosen People's African Name deny the name Nigga as the ancestral name of our Heavenly Father, and

(2) The Ills of our Creator's Chosen People's African Name repress Niggas as an actual Nation of People.

Verse 21

In combating the Powers of Evil within the Battlefields of a Negatively Induced Environment, the Spiritual Forces of Good deriving from within our Creator's Throne, saturated through the bloodline of our Creator's Chosen People to cultivate Niggas in their comprehensive development of living in accordance with our Creator's Universal Laws of Existence, to thereby alleviate the Misconceptions and dealing with the Ills of our Creator's Chosen People's African Name.

Precept A: Alleviating the Misconceptions

Verse 22

Now, despite all the Misconceptions about the meaning and origins of the "name," the name Nigga means Love, and the origins of the name *Nigga* come from Africa.

Verse 23

And it is our Creator's Chosen People's Cultural Family Name, named after our cultural Father who gave Life to Humankind as the First Man created.

Verse 24

But from the outset, let it be clarified that the Misconceptions that derive from the name *Nigga* come from the misuse and abuse of the name *Nigga* within the terms of another culture's language.

Verse 25

And by Satan attacking the Moralities of our Creator's Chosen People, the misconceptions about the meaning and origins of the name *Nigga* were intended to strategically turn African slave descendants away from embracing the Truth about their Origins – because a People without the knowledge of their True Origins are a People Ignorant and Incoherent to their own Heritage.

Verse 26

Wherefore, in alleviating the Misconceptions about the name Nigga, it must first be understood that not all African slave descendants are Niggas – because know that there were Africans who assisted the Europeans in the kidnapping and enslavement of Niggas, due to the fact that they "opposed" the Ruling Authority of our Heavenly Father.

Verse 27

And the bloodline of those Africans who hated Niggas as a People became the descendants who have wholeheartedly adopted the name *Negro* as the cultural name for all African slave descendants, whereby executing an evil scheme to consequently bring a demise to the Heritage of Niggas being our Creator's Chosen People.

Verse 28

And those so-called *Negros* are actually our Creator's Chosen People's Worst Enemy, due to the fact that they have shown to ally with the Forces of Evil within the Battlefields of a negatively induced environment – thereby infiltrating the leadership of our Creator's Chosen People.

Verse 29

Because instead of steering the African slave descendants toward becoming an independent African Nation, those so-called *Negros* consciously made the decision to integrate with the wicked Nation who killed and enslaved Africans – whereby leading all African slave descendants to become submissive to an Evil European/American Rule that continues to Persecute Niggas.

Verse 30

And although many African slave descendants have profited from integrating with this Evil American Nation, at the End-time of Satan's Dominion upon the Earth's living – the people who have promoted and profited from demoralizing the Qualities and Standards that exemplify the conduct of living in accordance with our Creator's Universal Laws of Existence, will be Blamed for the misguidance of our Creator's Chosen People and punished for allying with the Forces of Evil within the Battlefields of a negatively induced environment.

Verse 31

And let it be understood that the suffering Tribulations of the African slave descendants called Niggas were due to people opposing the Ruling Authority of our Heavenly Father, and regardless of the Misconceptions that derive from the name *Nigga* – to deny the name *Nigga* as the ancestral Name of our Heavenly Father is to oppose the Heritage of Niggas as our Creator's Chosen People.

Precept B: Dealing with the Ills

Verse 32

Now in comprehending the Ills that derive from the name Nigga, it is to be understood that when spoken within the cultural terms of an African tribal dialect, the name Nigga is used to express an endearment for the Glory of our cultural existence, in which it gives reverence to the Father of our African culture.

Verse 33

But when spoken within the terms and dialect of another tribe or cultural language, specifically Europeans, the terminology is Offensive because the usage of the name Nigga is taken out of its original context, thereby belittling the existence of our African culture as a Nation of People.

Verse 34

And this attack upon the cultural existence of Niggas as a Nation of People was predicated by a Satanic scheme that deceived the European nations to unite as one against our Creator's Chosen People in a conquest to Rule the entire world.

Verse 35

Because remember, the European culture is the people whose ancestors were responsible for the enslavement of Niggas and the destruction of our African Kingdom, which consequently makes the European culture Natural Enemies of our Creator's Chosen People.

Verse 36

And this explains why when a European uses the name Nigga out of its original context, this usage expresses the desire to make the African culture subordinate to the conquest of European rule.

Verse 37

And when the name Nigga is maliciously spoken from the tongue of a wicked European, its usage exposes that European's Hatred for the African culture and expresses that European's desire to continue to Persecute Niggas.

Verse 38

Wherefore, it is in dealing with the Ills that derive from the improper usage of the name Nigga, it must be clarified that just as not all African slave descendants are Niggas, not all Europeans are racist or wicked. But because of the misuse of the name Nigga and the mistreatment of all African slave descendants, if you are not a Nigga, then you are not allowed to interpret or use the name Nigga.

Verse 39

Because regardless of the meaning or origins of the name Nigga, these people who Hate the people who are called Niggas, they are unjust, and that hatred proves that there exists a culture of people who desire to continue to persecute Niggas. And at the end time of Satan's dominion upon the Earth's living, all those people who had maliciously used the name Nigga will be Shamed for the iniquities induced by the European invasion of Africa and punished for conspiring to prevent the fulfillment of our Creator's Divine Covenant with Humankind.

Verse 40

And let it be understood that although this Hatred and Persecution of Niggas was and is not righteously warranted, our Creator's Chosen People's ignorance of the stratagems of evil and their lack of Discipline and Unity as a culture still does not squander the fact that as a Nation of People, Niggas were responsible for upholding the Conditional Principles of our Creator's Spiritual Existence.

Verse 41

And so in substantiating the harsh fact that the African slave descendants called Niggas are our Creator's Chosen People, upon the Judicial proceedings for the Confrontation of Truth, the established comprehension of the name Nigga being the ancestral name of our Heavenly Father and the proven understanding of Niggas being an actual Nation of People, will be presented by our Heavenly Father divinely revealing who is the Messiah of Life.

Harsh Fact 2: The Blasphemy of Jesus Christ is the Manipulation that disguises Satan as God.

Verse 42

Now, at the time when Satan had formulated the Powers of Evil to structure the Spheres and Schemes of Evil Conductivity within all the Kingdoms of the Earth, the Powers of Evil had conceived the Birth of Jesus Christ – to thereby create the Religious Empire of Christianity.

Verse 43

And with the Birth of Jesus Christ, the Powers of Evil were able to "deceptively" enact the fulfillment of the Messianic Prophecies – which misled the followers of Christianity into believing that Jesus Christ was the Prophesied Messiah who was to establish God's everlasting Kingdom upon the Earth.

Verse 44

And with the teachings of Christianity, the Powers of Evil had also misled the followers of Christianity into promoting and supporting the Jewish culture as our Creator's Chosen People of God.

Verse 45

But in actuality, the Jewish People are not our Creator's Chosen People of God, and Jesus Christ was and is not the Prophesied Messiah who was to establish God's everlasting Kingdom upon the Earth.

Verse 46

In fact, this deception of Jesus Christ being the Prophesied Messiah who was to establish God's everlasting Kingdom upon the Earth is the Manipulation that fuels all the chaos and confusion that is going on within our world's living, because this Manipulation enabled Satan to disguise himself as God – to thereby use God's podium to promote and teach the Concept of an Unconditional Law of existing, while also allowing the Forces of Evil within the Battlefields of a negatively induced environment to disguise themselves as Servants of God, thereby roaming unnoticed and unpunished "to and fro" within the Kingdoms of the Earth, creating chaos and confusion.

Verse 47

And with this Manipulation, Satan was able to make the world believe that he does not exist within the "human form," while also deceiving the followers of Christianity into worshipping and praising him (Satan) as God – to thereby propel the Conductivity of Evil.

Verse 48

Because instead of teaching the people not to Sin and remain obedient to our Creator's (10) Ten Commandments, Christianity teaches its followers that with the crucifixion of Jesus Christ, whosoever believes in Jesus Christ as their Savior – they will be redeemed of their Sins and granted entrance into the Kingdom of Heaven to be given Eternal Life.

Verse 49

Which means that, no matter how many times a person commits a Sin, upon professing that Jesus Christ is the Prophesied Messiah and their Savior – they will be forgiven without consequence for their Sins committed.

Verse 50

And these teachings of Christianity are based upon the Concept of an Unconditional Law of existing, which allows Humankind to Sin without consequence upon their Appeal for Forgiveness.

Verse 51

But let it hereby be declared as the Absolute Truth that the name of Christ is the name of Satan and the Religion of Christianity is a Sanctuary for sinners.

Verse 52

And the evidential proof of Christ being Satan is established within the Symbol that represents Christ as God, which is the Cross.

Verse 53

Because understand, God is Love, and Love in action creates Life, and if a Symbol is to represent God – it would represent Love, and the use of the symbol would reflect upon producing Life.

Verse 54

And in contrast, Satan is Hatred, and Hatred in action produces Death, and if a Symbol is to represent Satan – it would represent Hatred, and the use of the Symbol would reflect upon producing Death.

Verse 55

And now, if we look at the Cross, it is a Symbol that represents Hatred and Torment, as the use of the Cross reflects upon producing Death – because the Cross was an instrument used to crucify and kill people.

Verse 56

And to honor Jesus Christ as the Prophesied Messiah who is to establish God's everlasting Kingdom upon the Earth and to acknowledge the Cross as the Symbol of God would be to say that a Man-made instrument used to crucify and kill people – subdued the Powers of our Creator, thereby bringing Death upon the Person of God.

Verse 57

And furthermore, Evidence of Jesus Christ not being the Prophesied Messiah who is to establish God's everlasting Kingdom upon the Earth is documented within the scriptures of the Bible as the recordings of his Last Words before his Death upon the Cross – which were, "Father, Why have you forsaken me?"

Verse 58

Wherein the Last Words describe Jesus Christ as being Forsaken by our Heavenly Father, and if Jesus Christ was the Prophesied Messiah who was to establish God's everlasting Kingdom upon the Earth, then our Heavenly Father would not have forsaken him – due to the fact that the Prophesied Messiah of Life is the One begotten Son of our Heavenly

Father who is born of Humankind to be the Crowned King of Heaven; and it is the Birth and fulfilled prophecy of the Messiah of Life which will solidify the embodiment of our Creator's Spiritual Existence within Humankind's creation as Everlasting.

Verse 59

And to fulfill the prophecy, the Messiah of Life must establish God's everlasting Kingdom upon the Earth – which means that the Prophesied Messiah of Life will institute an undertaking course of Universal Resurrection, which will lead Humankind from the Negative Realities of living upon the Earth to the Positive Realities of living in accord with the Kingdom of Heaven.

Verse 60

And during this undertaking course of Universal Resurrection, the Prophesied Messiah of Life will sit upon our Creator's Throne as our Heavenly Father's Crowned King of Heaven – and he will protect the Righteous and punish the Wicked, thereby sustaining the Judicial Qualifications and Jurisdictions that will uphold Universal Justice.

Verse 61

But in his first coming, Jesus Christ did not establish God's everlasting Kingdom upon the Earth, nor did he institute an undertaking course to a Positive Reality for Humankind to follow – so what evidence do Christians have that proves

Jesus Christ will establish God's everlasting Kingdom upon the Earth in his so-called "second coming"?

Verse 62

And if Jesus Christ had died and went to Heaven to sit upon our Creator's Throne as the Crowned King of Heaven, then why has Jesus Christ not protected the Righteous and punished the Wicked – and why is there so much Injustice, Corruption, Suffering, and Violence going on in our world's living?

Verse 63

Whereas the Truth of the matter is that Jesus Christ was and is not the Prophesied Messiah of Life as proclaimed by the Religion of Christianity – because Jesus Christ is actually the Messiah of Death, whose duties are to deceive the People of the Earth into becoming consensual with living in accordance with an Unconditional Law of existing, whereby to lure as many People into an Eternal Existence of Death with him.

Verse 64

And as for the Jewish culture being our Creator's Chosen People of God, these understandings were intentionally misinterpreted to promote Satan's Stratagem – because the Hebrew Nationality was assigned to protect the prophecy of the Messiah as an agreement to validate the Conditional Realities of our Creator's Spiritual Existence within their "ancestral" creation, in whom, while protecting the prophecy of the Messiah, did have Jesus Christ crucified for his blasphemy.

Verse 65

And so, in substantiating the harsh fact that the Blasphemy of Jesus Christ is the Manipulation that disguises Satan as God, upon the Judicial proceedings for the Confrontation of Truth – the Personification of Satan will be apprehended and summoned by our Creator's Omnipotent Court of Universal Law to thereby object -or- confirm the Testimony of the One whom our Heavenly Father is divinely revealing as the Messiah of Life.

Harsh Fact 3: Satan's Stratagem within the Spiritual Conflict between Good and Evil was to Attack The Moralities of our Creator's Chosen People.

Verse 66

Now, to produce the Trial Evidence needed to prove that living in accordance with an Unconditional Law of existing is "More Pleasurable" than living in accordance with our Creator's Universal Laws of Existence, Satan must discredit our Creator's Divine Covenant with Humankind by preventing the embodied (Re) Creation of our Creator's Spiritual Existence borne of our Creator's Chosen People – in whom is the Messiah of Life, from establishing the Direction and Disposition that will lead Humankind in the Universal Resurrection to a Positive Existence.

Verse 67

And to prevent the Messiah of Life from fulfilling our Creator's Divine Covenant with Humankind, Satan's Stratagem within the Spiritual Conflict between Good and Evil was to Attack the Moralities of our Creator's Chosen People, to thereby demonstrate the Forces of Evil that exist within the nature of Humankind's creation as being Stronger than the Spiritual Forces of Good deriving from within our Creator's Throne.

Verse 68

And by definition, the Moralities of our Creator's Chosen People are the Qualities of living within the Standards that exemplify the conduct of living in accordance with our Creator's Universal Laws of Existence.

Verse 69

And by attacking the Moralities of our Creator's Chosen People, the Undertaking Objective for the Forces of Evil within the Battlefields of a Negatively Induced Environment was to deter our Creator's Chosen People from upholding the Conditional Principles of our Creator's Spiritual Existence – in which are the Righteous Mode and Moral Standards that will maintain the Conductivity that produces the Positive Energies of a Universal Desire to Need to Live with the Love of our Creator as the Crowned King of Heaven.

Verse 70

And so, from the execution of Satan's Stratagem, the Undertaking Combat to overcome the Forces of Evil within the Battlefields of a Negatively Induced Environment came to be the Struggles of Survival that our Creator's Chosen People faced against the Rule of an American Nation.

Verse 71

Because this American Nation is actually the Facade that allowed the Powers of Evil to establish the objective understandings to the Pleasures of living in accordance with an Unconditional Law of existing – which, in fact, manipulates the People to Stand for the Wrongs of an Evil Existence.

Verse 72

And from the Rule of this American Nation, the Powers of Evil had strategically attacked:

(1) *the Physical Well-Being of Niggas* by forcing our Creator's Chosen People to submit to the governing order of a European conquest through the techniques of Slavery and Racism, and

(2) *the Mental Stability of Niggas* by concealing from our Creator's Chosen People the Knowledge of their True Origins through the designs of Brainwashing the People with Negative Entertainment and Unsound Philosophies, and

(3) *the Spiritual Beliefs of Niggas* by making our Creator's Chosen People lose self-esteem and become despaired through the disguises of Seducing the People into worshipping Desolated Images and Fallacious Livelihoods.

Verse 73

And by keeping our Creator's Chosen People trapped within a Slave Mentality, Satan's evil scheme was to restrict Niggas from mentally grasping the understandings of their own inherent Strengths and Abilities – thereby enabling the Forces of Evil within the Battlefields of a Negatively Induced Environment to influence our Creator's Chosen People into abandoning the obligations and duties that bind them to their Heritage.

Verse 74

Because of strategically attacking the Physical Well-Being, Mental Stability, and Spiritual Beliefs of our Creator's Chosen People, the Powers of Evil believed that the results would perpetuate the chaos and confusion that would deter our Creator's Chosen People from upholding the Conditional Principles of our Creator's Spiritual Existence.

Verse 75

And to deter our Creator's Chosen People from upholding the Conditional Principles of our Creator's Spiritual Existence, that would bring about the theological Death of our Creator's Chosen People in the form of not allowing the Spiritual Forces of Good to reach their Greatest Potential –

thereby demonstrating the Forces of Evil that exist within the nature of Humankind's creation as being stronger than the Spiritual Forces of Good deriving from within our Creator's Throne.

Verse 76

And for the Spiritual Forces of Good to not reach their "Greatest Potential," that would mean that the embodied (Re)Creation of our Creator's Spiritual Existence borne of our Creator's Chosen People would have failed to establish the Direction and Disposition that would lead Humankind in the Universal Resurrection to a Positive Existence, thereby discrediting our Creator's Divine Covenant with Humankind.

Verse 77

And to discredit our Creator's Divine Covenant with Humankind, that would make God out to be a Liar, thereby producing the Trial Evidence needed to prove Satan's Claim that living in accordance with an Unconditional Law of existing is "More Pleasurable" than living in accordance with our Creator's Universal Laws of Existence.

Verse 78

And so, in substantiating the harsh fact that Satan's Stratagem within the Spiritual Conflict between Good and Evil was to attack the Moralities of our Creator's Chosen People, it will be during the Judicial proceedings for the Confrontation of Truth when our Creator's Omnipotent

Court of Universal Law will subpoena Satan to testify to the Evil schemes and Forces that influenced many of our Creator's Chosen People into abandoning the obligations and duties that bind them to their Heritage.

Harsh Fact 4: The Moralities of our Creator's Chosen People were defended by the Gangster Disciples, Standardizing the Measures for living in accordance with our Creator's Universal Laws of Existence.

Verse 79

Now, our Creator understood that the Satanic attacks upon the Moralities of our Creator's Chosen People had to be defended because the Qualities of living within the Standards that exemplify the conduct of living in accordance with our Creator's Universal Laws of Existence must be instilled within the nature of our Creator's Chosen People – thereby producing the embodied (Re)Creation of our Creator's Spiritual Existence from within their bloodline.

Verse 80

And by definition, our Creator's Universal Laws of Existence are the established Principles that maintain the proper Code of Conduct in which to sustain the Conditional Realities of our Creator's Spiritual Existence within creation.

Verse 81

And upon the European invasion of Africa, our Creator knew that in time – living within the Battlefields of a negatively induced environment would produce the negative comprehensions that would mislead our Creator's Chosen People from the Righteous Qualities and Moral Behavior needed to sustain the Conditional Realities of our Creator's Spiritual Existence within creation.

Verse 82

And so, in the Beginning, it was strategized by our Creator that After the timely Death of the First Man created – in whom was our Creator's Chosen People's ancestral King, the Spiritual Forces of Good deriving from within our Creator's Throne would saturate through the bloodline of our Creator's Chosen People's tribal communities, thereby cultivating our Creator's Chosen People in their comprehensive development of living in accordance with our Creator's Universal Laws of Existence.

Verse 83

And from this cultivation, the strong Faithful descendants of our Creator's Chosen People who rebelled against the Rule of the American Nation – they will:

(1) embody the Mobilization of the Spiritual Forces of Good within the Struggles of Survival for our Creator's Chosen People, and

(2) serve as the Militant Units that will defend the Moralities of our Creator's Chosen People, and

(3) come to be known as the Brothers and Sisters of the Struggle in whom will uphold the Conditional Principles of our Creator's Spiritual Existence, to thereby Standardize the Measures for living in accordance with our Creator's Universal Laws of Existence.

Verse 84

And this saturation of the Spiritual Forces of Good cultivating our Creator's Chosen People in their comprehensive development of living in accordance with our Creator's Universal Laws of Existence was ascribed by our Creator as the Beginning Interconnection of perfecting the development of Humankind's creation.

Verse 85

And by definition, the Measures for living in accordance with our Creator's Universal Laws of Existence are the "course of action" that fulfills the obligations and duties required in maintaining the proper Code of Conduct in which to sustain the Conditional Realities of our Creator's Spiritual Existence within creation.

Verse 86

And from the Mobilization of the Spiritual Forces of Good combating against the Forces of Evil within the Battlefields of a Negatively Induced Environment, the conduct of upholding the Conditional Principles of our Creator's

Spiritual Existence had Standardized the Measures for living in accordance with our Creator's Universal Laws of Existence – to thereby guide Humankind in adjusting to and conforming with the provisions and proportions set for acquiring the Qualities and Standards needed to maintain the constant activation of the Energies of Love.

Verse 87

Because by our Creator's Chosen People upholding the Conditional Principles of our Creator's Spiritual Existence while combating against the Forces of Evil within the Battlefields of a Negatively Induced Environment, the Righteous Qualities and Moral Behavior needed to sustain the Conditional Realities of our Creator's Spiritual Existence within creation will also establish the Righteous Mode and Moral Standards in which will maintain the Conductivity that produces the Positive Energies of a Desire to Need to Live with the Love of our Creator as the Crowned King of Heaven.

Verse 88

And it was in "Standardizing" the Measures for living in accordance with our Creator's Universal Laws of Existence that the most specialized Militant Unit within the Spiritual Forces of Good – known as the Gangster Disciples, produced the Blueprint of Growth and Development.

Verse 89

And by definition, the Blueprint of Growth and Development is the designed concept and ideology of organization which stimulates membership application in the direction of living in accordance with our Creator's Universal Laws of Existence.

Verse 90

And as strategized by our Creator, in the End-time of Satan's (6) six-thousand years of Dominion upon the Earth's living – the Mobilization of the Spiritual Forces of Good had employed from the Gangster Disciples, the Divine Will-Power to institute the Stabilizing Measures for balancing the Equilibrium to living within our Creator's Universal Existence of One Love.

Verse 91

And this Divine Will-Power was produced by the embodied (Re) Creation of our Creator's Spiritual Existence borne of our Creator's Chosen People, in whom by the embodiment to the Divine Entity of One Love and the prescription for the Mobilization to the Institutions of Universal Peace, has established the Disposition and Direction that will lead Humankind in the Universal Resurrection to a Positive Existence – thereby fulfilling our Creator's Divine Covenant with Humankind.

Verse 92

Hence, it is the standardization of the Measures for living in accordance with our Creator's Universal Laws of Existence that is transcribed by our Creator to be the Ending Interconnection of perfecting the development of Humankind's creation – while the institution of the Stabilizing Measures for balancing the Equilibrium to living within our Creator's Universal Existence of One Love will be prescribed by our Creator as the Completing Process of perfecting the development of Humankind's creation.

Verse 93

And so in substantiating the harsh fact that the Moralities of our Creator's Chosen People were defended by the Gangster Disciples "standardizing" the Measures for living in accordance with our Creator's Universal Laws of Existence, upon the Judicial proceedings for the Confrontation of Truth – the Spiritual Forces of Good in Mobilizing the Institutions of Universal Peace onto the Kingdoms of the Earth, will install the System of Growth and Development as the Infrastructure for Universal Peace.

Verse 94

And in conclusion, by acknowledging these (4) four harsh facts as the Realities of Truth, Humankind will come to understand the "Reckoning Disposition of our Creator's Omnipotent Court of Universal Law" – thereby establishing the Disposition needed to overcome the Evil that exists within the nature of their creation.

Verse 95

Because upon acknowledging these (4) four harsh facts as the Realities of Truth, a person will initiate the process of producing and developing the habitual tendencies that will Stand with the Spiritual Forces of Good in subduing the Energies of a Negative Existence for Humankind's Universal Resurrection to a Positive Existence.

CHAPTER SEVEN: THE RECKONING DISPOSITION OF OUR CREATOR'S OMNIPOTENT COURT OF UNIVERSAL LAW

Verse 1

Now, by definition, the Reckoning Disposition of our Creator's Omnipotent Court of Universal Law is the Legal Stance taken by the Love of our Creator in sustaining the Judicial Jurisdictions needed to settle the Spiritual Conflict between Good and Evil.

Verse 2

And in sustaining the Judicial Jurisdictions needed to settle the Spiritual Conflict between Good and Evil, the Love of our Creator, while overcoming the Powers of Evil within the Battlefields of a negatively induced environment, had progressively assumed the Authority that transcribed:

(1) the Summary of Judgment for the Spiritual Conflict between Good and Evil, in which summarizes the Stance that rejects Satan's

Claim that living in accordance with an Unconditional Law of existing is "More Pleasurable" than living in accordance with our Creator's Universal Laws of Existence,

(2) the Ruling Measures of the Absolute, in which details the Divine Requisitions for the undertaking course taken to determine the class-destinations within our Creator's Universal Existence of One Love, and

(3) the Measured Decree for the Judgment of True Love, in which ascribes the sequential order of the vindicated action taken by our Creator's Omnipotent Court of Universal Law in affirming the perfected development of each person's creation.

Verse 3

And with this Reckoning Disposition of our Creator's Omnipotent Court of Universal Law, the Love of our Creator will calibrate Balancing the Equilibrium to living within our Creator's Universal Existence of One Love – in which to guide Humankind in aligning and conforming with the Qualities and Standards of living in accordance with our Creator's Universal Laws of Existence.

Section 1: The Summary of Judgment for the Spiritual Conflict between Good and Evil

Verse 4

Now, upon making the Claim that living in accordance with an Unconditional Law of existing would be "More Pleasurable" than living in accordance with our Creator's Universal Laws of Existence, it is the Stance taken by Satan that – if a person errs and commits an act of Sin, that person should not have to Surely Die, especially since the Person of God, who is the established Authority of our Creator's Spiritual Existence within creation, has the Power to forgive them without consequence; in which Satan also contends that God's Love for Humankind should be Unconditional, to thereby fully express God's Desire to Need to Live with Humankind.

Verse 5

But for the Due Process of settling the Spiritual Conflict between Good and Evil, it is the Stance taken by the Love of our Creator that – the ideology and understandings of God's Love and/or any person's Love being Unconditional is a grave Misconception, because Love in itself is Conditional due to the fact that in order to truly "Desire to Need to Live" with another person, each person must fulfill the requirements and obligations that sustain the Conditions of Trust and Respect.

Verse 6

Whereto, it is the Conditions of Trust and Respect in which establish the Bond that solidifies a person's Desire to Need to Live with another person, for instance:

(1) in order for a Wife or a Husband to solidify their Love for their Spouse, they must fulfill the requirements and obligations needed to validate their Commitment – such as being Faithful and Cooperative as Partners in Life,

(2) in order for a Parent to solidify their Love for their Child, they must fulfill the requirements and obligations needed to Raise the Child – such as feeding, clothing, and nurturing the Child,

(3) in order for a Child to solidify their Love for their Parents, they must fulfill the requirements and obligations needed to Honor their Parents – such as being Obedient and Submissive to the proper Guidance of their Parents, and

(4) in order for a Brother or a Sister to solidify their Love for their Sibling, they must fulfill the requirements and obligations needed to uphold their Family Heritage – such as being their Brother's or Sister's Keeper.

Verse 7

And it is the fulfillment of these requirements and obligations in which sustains the Conditions of the Trust and Respect needed to create a Bond that solidifies a person's Desire to Need to Live with another person; and therefrom, the Conditions of Trust and Respect – the Bond of Love will grow and become stronger.

Verse 8

But more importantly, in order to live within the United Kingdoms of Heaven and Earth, the requirements and obligations that sustain the Conditions of Trust and Respect between God and Humankind must be fulfilled – to thereby establish the Bond that will solidify God's Love and Humankind's Desire to Need to Live with one another as One Universal Family.

Verse 9

Because in order for God to solidify His Love for Humankind, God must fulfill the requirements and obligations needed to maintain Humankind's Everlasting Life – such as Securing and Governing Humankind's Universal Existence.

Verse 10

And in order for Humankind to solidify their love for God, they must fulfill the requirements and obligations needed to glorify the creation of our Creator's existence – such as worshipping God and obeying our Creator's Universal Laws of Existence.

Verse 11

But by living in accordance with an Unconditional Law of existing, neither God nor Humankind can solidify their love for one another because committing acts of sin violates the conditions of trust and respect.

Verse 12

And to live within the United Kingdoms of Heaven and Earth as one Universal Family, if one person errs and commits a sinful act that violates the conditions of trust and respect against another person – then that person not only breaks the bond that solidifies their desire to need to live with the person whom they initially violated the conditions of trust and respect against, but they also break their bond of love with all the people living within our Universal Existence; including with God.

Verse 13

Because as a people living within a Universal Existence together as one Universal Family – if you violate the conditions of trust and respect with one person, then you violate the conditions of trust and respect with us all, and it is God's responsibility to secure our Universal Existence from the Conductivity of Evil "by governing Humankind's living to not commit acts of sin."

Verse 14

And for God to simply forgive and excuse a person of a Sinful act without consequence, that would be unjust because other people have already suffered as a result of the Negative energies that were produced from the Sinful act that that person had committed.

Verse 15

And also, regardless of how small or great the Sin committed is – if God forgives and excuses one person for a Sinful act without consequence, then in all righteousness, God will have to excuse and forgive every person living within our Universal Existence of a sinful act without consequence; whereby will one Sin then become a multitude of Sins.

Verse 16

And by forgiving and excusing all of Humankind living within our Universal Existence for any and all sinful acts committed without consequence, the multitude of the sinful acts committed will produce a magnetic force that will induce the evil that exists within the nature of Humankind's creation to "continuously engage in the Conductivity of Evil"; and this disables God from fulfilling the requirements and obligations needed to maintain Humankind's Everlasting Life.

Verse 17

Because Humankind continuously engaging in the Conductivity of Evil, subsequently propels the induced negative energies of a Universal Desire to Need to Live "without" the Person of God as the established Authority of our Creator's Spiritual Existence – whereby perpetuating the physical properties of our Creator's Universal Existence to operate within the Realities of a Negative Existence.

Verse 18

But in order to prove to Humankind that committed acts of sin can not be forgiven and excused without consequence, our Creator had permitted the Cause and Effects of Sin to take its course – whereby to allow Humankind to experience a living in accordance with an Unconditional Law of existing.

Verse 19

And so now as a result of Humankind living in accordance with an Unconditional Law of existing, the conduct deriving from the induced negative energies of a Universal Desire to Need to Live without the person of God as the established authority of our Creator's Spiritual Existence – had become embedded within Humankind's nature as the Will to Lust, Lie, Hate and Kill; and this disables Humankind from fulfilling the requirements and obligations needed to glorify the creation of our Creator's existence.

Verse 20

And with Humankind having the Will to Lust, Lie, Hate and Kill embedded within their nature, to forgive and excuse Humankind for the multitude of Sins committed without consequences will only promote Humankind to continuously engage in the Conductivity of Evil – whereby producing within the Kingdoms of the Earth, the Actualities of Chaos, Confusion, Misery and Death; in which perpetuates Humankind's living within the Realities of a Negative Existence.

Verse 21

And it is the Actualities of Chaos, Confusion, Misery and Death that are produced within the Kingdoms of the Earth in which becomes the Determining Evidence that weighs the "pleasurable circumstances" of how Humankind is living in accordance with an Unconditional Law of existing.

Verse 22

From this Determining Evidence, it is the opinion of our Creator's Omnipotent Court of Universal Law to support the Stance taken by the Love of our Creator, who maintains that—due to the Actualities of Chaos, Confusion, Misery, and Death produced within the Kingdoms of the Earth—a living in accordance with an Unconditional Law of existing is Not More Pleasurable than living in accordance with our Creator's Universal Laws of Existence. And this is the Summary of Judgment for the Spiritual Conflict between Good and Evil.

Section 2: The Ruling Measures of the Absolute

Verse 23

Now, in sustaining the Judicial Jurisdictions needed to settle the Spiritual Conflict between Good and Evil, the Ruling Measures of the Absolute are distinctly transcribed by the Love of our Creator, thereby establishing the Just Precedents for determining the class-destinations within our Creator's Universal Existence of One Love.

Verse 24

By definition, the Ruling Measures of the Absolute are the Divine Requisitions for the undertaking course of action taken to determine the class-destinations within our Creator's Universal Existence of One Love.

Verse 25

As designed, the class-destinations within our Creator's Universal Existence of One Love are the Occupations of our Creator's Spiritual Existence, functioning through Humankind's creation to stabilize the Circuitry that sustains the illumination of our Creator's Light.

Verse 26

In determining the class-destinations within our Creator's Universal Existence of One Love, Humankind must fulfill the qualified status placement for the Divine Requisitions of:

(1) Being proven Worthy of sitting upon our Creator's Throne as the Crowned King of Heaven,

(2) Being proven Worthy of occupancy within the Kingdom of Heaven to be or receive a Crown of Glory, and/or

(3) Being proven Worthy of occupancy within the Kingdoms of the Earth to be or receive a Crown of Life.

Verse 27

From these Divine Requisitions for the undertaking course of action taken to determine the class-determinations within our Creator's Universal Existence of One Love, the Virtuous Capacity for the activated Energies of Love within Humankind's creation will be assessed—thereby "Occupationally Placing" each person within the designed configuration that will induce the Positive Energies needed to sustain the illumination of our Creator's Light.

Verse 28

In correlation with establishing the Divine Entity of One Love, the Ruling Measures of the Absolute will interconnect the "Beginning process" that conceived the development of Humankind's creation (the Alpha), with the "Ending process" that perceives the development of Humankind's creation (the Omega)—to thereby formulate the "Completing process" that perfects the development of Humankind's creation (the Absolute).

Subsection A: The Divine Requisition for Being Proven Worthy of Sitting Upon Our Creator's Throne as the Crowned King of Heaven

Verse 29

The Divine Requisition for being proven Worthy of sitting upon our Creator's Throne as the Crowned King of Heaven was enacted by our Creator's Motion to Remand Satan onto the Kingdoms of the Earth, thereby producing the Trial Evidence needed to prove Satan's Claim that living in accordance with an Unconditional Law of existing is "More Pleasurable" than living in accordance with our Creator's Universal Laws of Existence.

Verse 30

By our Creator giving Satan approximately six thousand years of Dominion upon the Earth's living to instituted a living in accordance with an Unconditional Law of existing – this undertaking course of action was our Creator's

Omnipotent Court of Universal Law-prescribed process of establishing the Battlefields of a negatively induced environment within the Kingdoms of the Earth.

Verse 31

Because in order to produce the Trial Evidence needed to prove Satan's Claim that living in accordance with an Unconditional Law of existing is "More Pleasurable" than living in accordance with our Creator's Universal Laws of Existence, Satan must discredit our Creator's Divine Covenant with Humankind by preventing the embodied (Re) Creation of our Creator's Spiritual Existence borne of our Creator's Chosen People from establishing the Direction and Disposition that will lead Humankind in the Universal Resurrection to a Positive Existence.

Verse 32

And establishing the Battlefields of a negatively induced environment within the Kingdoms of the Earth enabled Satan to teach and influence Humankind to live in accordance with an Unconditional Law of existing— embedding within Humankind's nature the Evil habitual tendencies and qualities that deviate from the Righteous Principles and Moral Standards of living in accordance with our Creator's Universal Laws of Existence.

Verse 33

It was Satan's Stratagem to utilize the Battlefields of a negatively induced environment to deter our Creator's

Chosen People from upholding the Conditional Principles of our Creator's Spiritual Existence. Ultimately, Satan aimed to influence the embodied (Re) Creation of our Creator's Spiritual Existence borne of our Creator's Chosen People to deviate from the obligations and responsibilities of fulfilling our Creator's Divine Covenant with Humankind—thus producing the Trial Evidence needed to prove Satan's Claim that living in accordance with an Unconditional Law of existing is "More Pleasurable" than living in accordance with our Creator's Universal Laws of Existence.

Verse 34

Because Satan's objective was that, "If" living in accordance with an Unconditional Law of existing is *Not More Pleasurable* than living in accordance with our Creator's Universal Laws of Existence, then the embodied (Re) Creation of our Creator's Spiritual Existence borne of our Creator's Chosen People— while living within the Realities of a Negative Existence— should be able to resist immoral temptations and combat against the Powers of Evil within the Battlefields of a negatively induced environment, to thereby establish the Direction and Disposition that will lead Humankind in the Universal Resurrection to a Positive Existence, whereby becoming proven worthy of sitting upon our Creator's Throne as the Crowned King of Heaven.

Verse 35

Wherefore, it is the embodied (Re) Creation of our Creator's Spiritual Existence borne of our Creator's

Chosen People establishing the Divine Entity of One Love and designing the Mobilization of the Institutions of Universal Peace – in which fulfills the qualified status placement for the Divine Requisitions of being proven worthy of sitting upon our Creator's Throne as the Crowned King of Heaven, whereinto establishing the Beginning Interconnection of perfecting Humankind's creation.

Subsection B: Divine Requisition for Being Proven Worthy of Occupancy within the Kingdom of Heaven as to Be or Receive a Crown of Glory

Verse 36

The Divine Requisition for being proven Worthy of occupancy within the Kingdom of Heaven as to be or receive a Crown of Glory is enacted by our Creator's Motion to Suppress Satan's Allegation that God makes restrictions that limit the Potentials of other creations, whereby Satan was given the opportunity to Rule within the Kingdoms of the Earth without the established Authority of our Creator's Spiritual Existence within Humankind's creation.

Verse 37

And by our Creator closing the Gates of Heaven and ordering all who resided within the Kingdom of Heaven (including the Person of God) to embark upon the legal proceedings to settle the Spiritual Conflict between Good and Evil – this undertaking course of action was our Creator's Omnipotent Court of Universal Law instituting the procedure of processing the Undertaking Combat between the Spiritual Forces of Good and the Forces of Evil.

Verse 38

Because in the first (4) four thousand years of Satan's Dominion, while the Kingdoms of the Earth were being cultivated and the Battlefields of a negatively induced environment were being established – our Creator's Chosen People's African Kingdom was protected from the Conductivity of Evil, due to the fact that the First Man created (in whom was the Person of God), continued to exist as the established Authority of our Creator's Spiritual Existence within Humankind's creation; and these first (4) four thousand years of Satan's Dominion were recorded as the time Before Christ (B.C.).

Verse 39

But in the time After the Death of the First Man created, the Powers of Evil began dating the years of Satan's Rule within the Kingdoms of the Earth "without" the established Authority of our Creator's Spiritual Existence within Humankind's creation; and these last (2) two thousand years of Satan's Dominion were recorded as the Anno Domini (A.D.).

Verse 40

And in the years of Satan's Rule within the Kingdoms of the Earth "without" the established Authority of our Creator's Spiritual Existence within Humankind's creation, our

Creator's Chosen People's African Kingdom was no longer
protected from the Conductivity of Evil – because for the
Due Process of settling the Spiritual Conflict between Good
and Evil, the Struggles of Survival for our Creator's Chosen
People processed the Undertaking Combat between the
Spiritual Forces of Good and the Forces of Evil within the
Battlefields of a Negatively Induced Environment.

Verse 41

And it was established that this Undertaking Combat within
the Battlefields of a negatively induced environment will
give all of Humankind the opportunity to measure their own
Potentials of being proven Worthy of living within the
Kingdom of Heaven.

Verse 42

And from the Undertaking Combat within the Battlefields of
a Negatively Induced Environment, the Undertaking
Objective for:

(1) *the Powers of Evil* - is to "discredit" our Creator's Divine
Covenant with Humankind by demonstrating the Forces of
Evil that exist within the nature of Humankind's creation as
being stronger than the Spiritual Forces of Good deriving
from within our Creator's Throne.

(2) *our Creator's Chosen People* - is to sustain the Righteous
Mode and Moral Standards that will maintain the
Conductivity that produces the Positive Energies of a
Universal Desire to Need to Live with the Love of our

Creator as the Crowned King of Heaven, to thereby enable our Creator to (Re) Create from their bloodline – the embodied creation of our Creator's Spiritual Existence, in whom will fulfill our Creator's Divine Covenant with Humankind, and

(3) *those People who formulate the different Nationalities of the World* - is to sustain the actual Righteous Qualities and Moral Behavior in which capacitates the Virtues that allow the activated Energies of Love to remain in constant activation within the embodiment of their creation, to thereby reflect the Will-Power that observes our Creator's Universal Laws of Existence.

Verse 43

Wherefore, it is exemplifying the Image and Likeness of God while combating within the Battlefields of a Negatively Induced Environment – in which fulfills the qualified status placement for the Divine Requisition of being proven Worthy of occupancy within the Kingdom of Heaven as to be or receive a Crown of Glory, thereby establishing the Ending Interconnection of perfecting Humankind's creation.

Subsection C: The Divine Requisition for being Proven Worthy of Occupancy within the Kingdoms of the Earth as to be or receive a Crown of Life

Verse 44

The Divine Requisition for being proven Worthy of occupancy within the Kingdoms of the Earth as to be or receive a Crown of Life will be enacted by our Creator's Motion to Dismiss Satan's Claim that living in accordance with an Unconditional Law of existing is "More Pleasurable" than living in accordance with our Creator's Universal Laws of Existence, whereby to forever settle the Spiritual Conflict between Good and Evil.

Verse 45

And by our Creator closing the Gates of Heaven and ordering all who reside within the Kingdoms of the Earth to embark upon the Undertaking Combat within the Battlefields of a Negatively Induced Environment – this undertaking course of action was our Creator's Omnipotent Court of Universal Law ascribed process of evaluating Humankind's Desire to Need to Live with the Love of our Creator as our Heavenly Father's Crowned King of Heaven.

Verse 46

Because upon the End-time to Satan's (6) six thousand years of Dominion upon the Earth's Living, our Creator's Omnipotent Court of Universal Law will begin the Judicial proceedings for the Confrontation of Truth – in which time the embodied (RE) Creation of our Creator's Spiritual Existence borne from the blood lineage of our Creator's Chosen People will present Humankind with the Substantiated Evidence needed to be proven Worthy of sitting upon our Creator's Throne as our Heavenly Father's Crowned King of Heaven.

Verse 47

And it is the Substantiated Evidence of transcribing the Divine Entity of One Love and designing the Mobilization of the Institutions of Universal Peace, to thereby lead Humankind in the Universal Resurrection to a Positive Existence – in which will prove that the embodied (Re) Creation of our Creator's Spiritual Existence borne of our Creator's Chosen People is the Only One Worthy of sitting upon our Creator's Throne as our Heavenly Father's Crowned King of Heaven; thus establishing the "Beginning Interconnection" of perfecting Humankind's creation.

Verse 48

And upon being Vindicated by our Creator's Omnipotent Court of Universal Law as our Heavenly Father's "Anointed" Crowned King of Heaven, the embodied (Re) Creation of our Creator's Spiritual Existence borne of our Creator's Chosen People – in whom is the Love of our Creator, will move to Suppress Satan's Allegation that God makes restrictions that limit the Potentials of other creations.

Verse 49

And to Suppress Satan's Allegation that God makes restrictions that limit the Potentials of other creations, the Love of our Creator during the Judicial proceedings for the Confrontation of Truth will Court Womankind – in whom must by "Free Will" choose to either:

• submit to the Love of our Creator as our Heavenly Father's Crowned King of Heaven, or

• reject the Love of our Creator as our Heavenly Father's Crowned King of Heaven.

Verse 50

And from the enactment of Suppressing Satan's Allegation that God makes restrictions that limit the Potentials of other creations, our Creator's Omnipotent Court of Universal Law will Open the Gates of Heaven to ascend the Love of our Creator onto our Creator's Throne – whereby to commence "the Marriage Ceremony for the Love of our Creator."

Verse 51

And thereupon the Opening of the Gates of Heaven, all those People who are proven Worthy of sitting upon our Creator's Throne and proven Worthy of occupancy within the Kingdom of Heaven as to be or receive a Crown of Glory, they will become Vindicated by our Creator's Omnipotent Court of Universal Law and gathered to be Blessed-In Marriage with the Love of our Creator – and all those People who knowingly and intentionally opposed and conspired against the Spiritual Forces of Good along with all those People who chose to reject the Love of our Creator as our Heavenly Father's Crowned King of Heaven, they will be Stricken by our Creator and gathered to be Cast into an Eternal Existence of Death with Satan; thus establishing the "Ending Interconnection" of perfecting Humankind's creation.

Verse 52

But every Person Not Vindicated by our Creator's Omnipotent Court of Universal Law during the Judicial proceedings for the Confrontation of Truth, who by Free Will chose to submit to the Love of our Creator as our Heavenly Father's Crowned King of Heaven – they will begin embarking upon the undertaking course to establish the Disposition that will overcome the Evil that exists within the nature of their creation; thus establishing the "Completing Process" of perfecting Humankind's creation.

Verse 53

Because thereafter Suppressing Satan's Allegation that God makes restrictions that limit the Potentials of other creations, our Creator's Omnipotent Court of Universal Law will then move to Dismiss Satan's Claim that living in accordance with an Unconditional Law of existing is "More Pleasurable" than living in accordance with our Creator's Universal Laws of Existence – whereby to begin the litigations that will determine who All are Worthy of occupancy within the Kingdoms of the Earth as to be or receive a Crown of Life.

Verse 54

And these litigations that will determine who all are Worthy of occupancy within the Kingdoms of the Earth as to be or receive a Crown of Life will be instituted for the Due Process of settling the Spiritual Conflict between Good and

Evil as the Universal Trial proceedings for the Judgment of True Love – in which manner must Humankind begin standardizing the Measures for living in accordance with our Creator's Universal Laws of Existence, whereby to balance the Equilibrium of living within our Creator's Universal Existence of One Love.

Verse 55

Wherefore, it is in adjusting to and conforming with the provisions and proportions set for acquiring the Qualities and Standards needed to maintain the constant activation of the Energies of Love in the allotted time established by our Creator's Omnipotent Court of Universal Law – in which fulfills the qualified status placement for the Divine Requisition of being proven Worthy of occupancy within the Kingdoms of the Earth as to be or receive a Crown of Life, wherein establishing the Completing process of perfecting Humankind's creation.

Section 3: The Measured Decree for the Judgment of True Love

Verse 56

Now by definition, the Measured Decree for the Judgment of True Love is the sequential order of the vindicated action taken by our Creator's Omnipotent Court of Universal Law in affirming the perfected development of each person's creation.

Verse 57

And in correlation with settling the Spiritual Conflict between Good and Evil, the Measured Decree for the Judgment of True Love will assess each person's virtuous capacity for the activated Energies of Love – based upon each person's attested Conquest from the Undertaking Combat within the Battlefields of a negatively induced environment.

Verse 58

And as such, it is the vindicating action taken by our Creator's Omnipotent Court of Universal Law in producing the occurrences of the Apocalypse for the reasons of initiating the Judicial proceedings for the Confrontation of Truth – in which divinely affirms that the One "Anointed" as our Heavenly Father's Crowned King of Heaven has overcome the Powers of Evil within the Battlefields of a negatively induced environment, to thereby move to Suppress Satan's Allegations that God makes restrictions that limit the Potentials of other creations.

Verse 59

And from the enactment of Suppressing Satan's Allegation that God makes restrictions that limit the Potentials of other creations, our Creator's Omnipotent Court of Universal Law will Open the Gates of Heaven – to thereby ascend the embodied (Re)Creation of our Creator's Spiritual Existence borne of our Creator's Chosen People, in whom is the Love of our Creator onto our Creator's Throne.

Verse 60

And therein ascending the Love of our Creator onto our Creator's Throne, our Creator will commence the observance of our Creator's Sacred Rites of Marriage with the Marriage Ceremony for the Love of our Creator – to thereby authorize the prescribed Order of Virtue for Humankind to begin receiving our Creator's Spiritual Blessings.

Verse 61

But before the commencement of the Marriage Ceremony for the Love of our Creator, those Women "during" the Judicial proceedings for the Confrontation of Truth whom by Free Will submitted to the Love of our Creator as our Heavenly Father's Crowned King of Heaven – they will be anointed as the Love from our Creator "upon" the opening of the Gates of Heaven, to thereby validate the established Fundamental Truth for the Glory of our Creator.

Verse 62

And as such, it is the vindicating action taken by our Creator's Omnipotent Court of Universal Law, in opening the Gates of Heaven to commence the Marriage Ceremony for the Love of our Creator – in which divinely affirms that the Spiritual Forces of Good have overcome the Forces of Evil within the Battlefields of a negatively induced environment, to thereby begin the Universal Trial proceedings for the Judgment of True Love.

Verse 63

And thereupon the Opening of the Gates of Heaven:

(1) Those Women proven Worthy of sitting upon our Creator's Throne as our Heavenly Father's Crowned Queens of Heaven, in the vindicating action taken by our Creator's Omnipotent Court of Universal Law – they will be gathered to ascend onto our Creator's Throne, to thereby partake in the Marriage Ceremony for the Love of our Creator as established by our Creator's Sacred Rites of Marriage, and

(2) Those People proven Worthy of occupancy within the Kingdom of Heaven as to be or receive a Crown of Glory, in the vindicating action taken by our Creator's Omnipotent Court of Universal Law – they will be gathered to enter the Kingdom of Heaven, to thereby become Blessed-In Marriage with the Love of our Creator as established by our Creator's Sacred Rites of Marriage, but

(3) Those People who knowingly and willfully allied and conspired with the Forces of Evil and those People who reject the Love of our Creator as our Heavenly Father's Crowned King of Heaven – they will be Stricken by our Creator and gathered to be cast into an Eternal Existence of Death, to thereby be Expatriated from living within our Creator's Universal Existence of One Love.

Verse 64

And thereafter the Judicial proceedings for the Confrontation of Truth, the Universal Trial proceedings for the Judgment of True Love will begin – in which instances will our Creator's Omnipotent Court of Universal Law adjudge the enactment of Dismissing Satan's Claim that living in accordance with an Unconditional Law of existing is "more pleasurable" than living in accordance with our Creator's Universal Laws of Existence.

Verse 65

And it is in Dismissing Satan's Claim that living in accordance with an Unconditional Law of existing is "more pleasurable" than living in accordance with our Creator's Universal Laws of Existence, must each Person who chose to submit to the Love of our Creator as our Heavenly Father's crowned King of Heaven – begin to Standardize the Measures for living in accordance with our Creator's Universal Laws of Existence, to thereby balance the Equilibrium to living within our Creator's Universal Existence of One Love.

Verse 66

And therein the Universal Trial proceedings for the Judgment of True Love:

(1) those People proven Worthy of occupancy within the Kingdoms of the Earth as to be or receive a Crown of Life, in the vindicating action taken by our Creator's Omnipotent Court of Universal Law – they will, in the appropriate time, be gathered to visit the Kingdom of Heaven, to thereby become Blessed-In Marriage with the Love of our Creator as established by our Creator's Sacred Rites of Marriage, but

(2) those People who violate the Settlement Orders of Peace with the Kingdom of Heaven and/or those People whose Equilibrium to living within our Creator's Universal Existence of One Love is not promptly balanced in the allotted time period established by our Creator's Omnipotent Court of Universal Law – they will be Stricken by our Creator and gathered to be cast into an Eternal Existence of Death, to thereby be Expatriated from living within our Creator's Universal Existence of One Love.

Verse 67

And this is the Measured Decree for the Judgment of True Love, as so ascribed by our Heavenly Father – the Supreme Justice of our Creator's Omnipotent Court of Universal Law.

Section 4: Balancing the Equilibrium to Living within Our Creator's Universal Existence of One Love

Verse 68

Now by Humankind living in accordance with an Unconditional Law of existing, there is no positive conditioning of Humankind's Universal conduct – and as a result, Humankind cannot produce or develop the habitual tendencies that will sustain the Energies of a Positive Existence.

Verse 69

And if a person cannot produce or develop the habitual

tendencies that sustain the Energies of a Positive Existence, then that person cannot be granted occupancy within the United Kingdoms of Heaven and Earth for an Everlasting Life living within our Creator's Universal Existence of One Love.

Verse 70

Because by definition, our Creator's Universal Existence of One Love is the everlasting Union of Heaven and Earth, in which our Creator's Spiritual Existence will forever exist within the embodiment of Humankind's creation – but to live within the United Kingdoms of Heaven and Earth, a person's Conduct and Livelihood must maintain the constant activation of the Energies of Love.

Verse 71

And so, upon living in accordance with an Unconditional Law of existing, in order for Humankind to live within the United Kingdoms of Heaven and Earth – Humankind must balance the Equilibrium to living within our Creator's Universal Existence of One Love.

Verse 72

And by definition:

(1) the Equilibrium to living within our Creator's Universal Existence of One Love is the balanced alignment and amends of conforming with the Qualities and Standards of living in accordance with our Creator's Universal Laws of Existence,

(2) the Qualities of living in accordance with our Creator's Universal Laws of Existence are the personal attributes and traits of righteous conduct in which enforces the constant activation of the Energies of Love, and

(3) the Standards of living in accordance with our Creator's Universal Laws of Existence are the Moral Requirements and Ethical Livelihoods that validate the Conditional Realities of our Creator's Spiritual Existence within Humankind's creation.

Verse 73

And to balance the Equilibrium to living within our Creator's Universal Existence of One Love, upon living in accordance with an Unconditional Law of existing – Humankind must adhere to "the Settlement Orders of Peace with the Kingdom of Heaven" and begin "Standardizing the Measures for living in accordance with our Creator's Universal Laws of Existence."

Subsection A: The Settlement Orders of Peace with the Kingdom of Heaven

Verse 74

Now, by definition, Peace is the absence of all Wars, Conflicts, and Hostilities – and upon Humankind living in accordance with an Unconditional Law of existing, Peace must be established through an agreement of a Settlement that maintains harmonious relations.

Verse 75

But to obtain harmonious relations with the Kingdom of Heaven upon living in accordance with an Unconditional Law of existing, each Person of the Earth must yield to the Progressive Direction of Growth and Development.

Verse 76

And by definition, the Progressive Direction of Growth and Development is the actual course of proceeding forward in living within our Creator's Universal Existence of One Love.

Verse 77

And it is in yielding to the Progressive Direction of Growth and Development that every Person living within the Kingdoms of Heaven and Earth must adhere to the following Settlement Orders:

(1) *Silence All Lies* - There will be No gossiping and/or lying to or about another person, and a person is to remain Silent if they cannot speak the Absolute Truth.

(2) *Drug and Alcohol* - No one is to consume or inject any controlled substance or intoxicant that is Not prescribed or allowed by the Authorities of our Creator's Throne.

(3) *Stealing* - No one is to take or possess the properties of another without the proper consent.

(4) Respect - No one is to disrespect another person in any shape, form, or fashion, and everyone must humbly practice

proper etiquette and mannerisms in adherence to our Creator's Universal Laws of Existence.

(5) *Trespass* - No one is to enter onto the properties or invade the Rights or Privacy of another person without the proper consent.

(6) Solicit and Gamble - No one is to entice or incite evil and/or unrighteous behavior, and no one is to make a bogus wage or act upon any mischievous undertaking of risk.

(7) *Gangster* - Everyone is subordinate to the Authoritative Direction of our Creator's G(s), and no one is to pretend nor Claim to be a G unless they are ordained or anointed as a G.

(8) *Sportsmanship* - No one is to cheat or engage in any unauthorized fight or argument as a result of playing any sport or game; everyone must practice good sportsmanship at all times.

(9) *Personal Hygiene* - Everyone is to keep their personal body, clothes, and living quarters clean at all times, and while in public, everyone must be appropriately dressed.

(10) *Incident* - All incidents, grievances, or suggestions must be reported to and dealt with accordingly by the proper authorities.

(11) *Aid and Assist* - Everyone is required to aid and assist one another in all righteous endeavors, however applicable – because we are our Brothers' and Sisters' Keepers.

(12) *Dues* - As Servants of God, everyone is required to give the proper dues and put forth their share of labor as revenue for the Utilities of our Creator's Universal Existence.

(13) *Diet and Exercise* - Everyone is to maintain a healthy diet and exercise as prescribed for each individual's physical fitness.

(14) *The Progressive Direction of Growth and Development* - Everyone must maintain Membership Admissions within the Institutions of Universal Peace and adhere to the authoritative decisions, commands, and orders for the proceeding course of living within our Creator's Universal Existence of One Love.

(15) *Exploitation* - No one is to use their position of authority, privilege, or favor to take advantage of anyone or to force anyone to do anything against their Free Will.

(16) *Fornication* - No one is to engage in any sexual practices or gratifications that are Not in pertinence with our Creator's Sacred Rites of Marriage.

(17) *Conflict* - No one is to entice or engage in any unrighteous encounters that can result in the physical, mental, or emotional maltreatment of another – everyone must strive to resolve all disagreements, issues, and/or problems.

Verse 78

And by adhering to these Settlement Orders of Peace with the Kingdom of Heaven, Humankind will proceed in

"Standardizing the Measures for living in accordance with our Creator's Universal Laws of Existence" – to thereby balance the Equilibrium of living within our Creator's Universal Existence of One Love.

Verse 79

But breach and transgression of these Settlement Orders of Peace with the Kingdom of Heaven will nullify that person's agreement to maintain their harmonious relations with the Kingdom of Heaven, and thereby will that person be Stricken by our Creator and gathered to be cast into an Eternal Existence of Death.

Subsection B: Standardizing the Measures for living in accordance with our Creator's Universal Laws of Existence

Verse 80

Now, by definition, Standardizing the Measures for living in accordance with our Creator's Universal Laws of Existence means to adjust to and conform with the provisions and proportions set for acquiring the Qualities and Standards needed to maintain the constant activation of the Energies of Love.

Verse 81

But upon Humankind living in accordance with an Unconditional Law of existing, in order to Standardize the Measures for living in accordance with our Creator's Universal Laws of Existence for Humankind's Universal

Resurrection to a Positive Existence – the Spiritual Forces of Good deriving from within our Creator's Throne must institute "the Stabilizing Measures for balancing the Equilibrium of living within our Creator's Universal Existence of One Love".

Verse 82

Because, by definition, the Stabilizing Measures for balancing the Equilibrium of living within our Creator's Universal Existence of One Love are the "Just Quantities" and "Actualities" to the course of action taken in adjusting to and conforming with the Qualities and Standards of living in accordance with our Creator's Universal Laws of Existence.

Verse 83

And to Standardize the Measures for living in accordance with our Creator's Universal Laws of Existence upon living in accordance with an Unconditional Law of existing:

(1) The "Just Quantities" for the Honorable Relations made by the individual in making Peace with the Kingdom of Heaven must be upheld, and

(2) The "Actualities" for the Dignified Interactions taken in keeping the Peace within the Kingdoms of the Earth must be applied.

Upholding the Just Quantities

Verse 84

Now, by definition, the Just Quantities that align a person's existence with the Qualities of living in accordance with our Creator's Universal Laws of Existence are the conducted and fulfilled obligations of a covenant, promise, and any agreement which upholds the Honorable Relations made by the individual within their personal course of action needed in making Peace with the Kingdom of Heaven.

Verse 85

And it is in upholding the Just Quantities that each person, upon their personal course of action needed in making Peace with the Kingdom of Heaven, must:

(1) Submit to the Authoritative Rule, Direction, and Command that is empowered from our Creator's Throne; and this will initiate the Trust that will define the Truth of a person's existence, thereby substantiating the Authenticity of that person's "Desire to Need to Live" with the Love of our Creator as our Heavenly Father's Crowned King of Heaven.

(2) Admit to the Misconceptions, Errors, and Transgressions that are recognized through the Teachings of Love; and this will process the Willingness to change and improve a person's existence, thereby evaluating the Integrity of that person's Will to Better Oneself.

(3) Commit to the Adjustments, Corrections, and Punishments that are administered by our Creator's Heavenly Body; and this will solidify the Wholeness that will uphold the Honorable Relations made by each person, thereby demonstrating their Worthiness to exist in Peace with the Kingdom of Heaven.

Verse 86

And by upholding the Just Quantities for the Honorable Relations made in making Peace with the Kingdom of Heaven, the personal attributes and traits of Righteous Conduct will characterize the Authenticity, Integrity, and Worthiness in which exhibit the Qualities that enforce the constant activation of the Energies of Love – thereby producing the Conduct that reflects the Image of God.

Applying the Actualities

Verse 87

Now, by definition, the Actualities that amends a person's behavior with the Standards of living in accordance with our Creator's Universal Laws of Existence are the complied and required duties of service, function, and any assigned task that execute the Dignified Interactions for the business course of action taken in keeping the Peace within the Kingdoms of the Earth.

Verse 88

And it is in applying the Actualities that each person, upon the business course of action taken in keeping the Peace within the Kingdoms of the Earth, must:

(1) Be Fruitful in the supplied Efforts of their employed Occupation, as a person's Labored Productivity will be ascertained by their Desire to Live as a positive, productive

person within the Kingdoms of Heaven and Earth; and this will display a person's Virtues.

(2) Multiply within the Market utilization of their certified Agreements, as the appraisal of a person's Prosperity will be determined by their Desire to Need an Esteemed Reputation; and this will confirm a person's Grace to live within our Creator's Universal Existence of One Love.

(3) Replenish the Earth with the calculated Savings of their implemented Services, as the Commissions that keep the Peace within the Kingdoms of the Earth will validate each person's Capacity to retain our Creator's Spiritual Blessings; and this will attest to a person's Respect for the established Authority of our Creator's Spiritual Existence.

Verse 89

And by applying the Actualities for the Dignified Interactions taken in keeping the Peace within the Kingdoms of the Earth accordingly, the Moral Requirements and Ethical Livelihoods will assess the Virtues, Grace, and Respect in which exhibit the Standards needed to validate the Conditional Realities of our Creator's Spiritual Existence within a person's creation – thereby developing the Livelihood that appreciates the Likeness of God.

Verse 90

And so, in conclusion, thereafter Suppressing Satan's Allegation that God makes restrictions that limit the Potentials of their creation – it is from the Reckoning Disposition of our Creator's Omnipotent Court of Universal Law, that our Creator's Omnipotent Court of Universal Law will move to Dismiss Satan's Claim that living in accordance with an Unconditional Law of existing is "More Pleasurable" than living in accordance with our Creator's Universal Laws of Existence.

Verse 91

And it is the Reckoning Disposition of our Creator's Omnipotent Court of Universal Law, adjudicated execution to Dismiss Satan's Claim through the Universal Trial proceedings for the Judgment of True Love that will settle the Spiritual Conflict between Good and Evil and formulate the Completing process that will perfect Humankind's creation – thereby completing the Procreation to the physical Properties of our Creator's Universal Existence while establishing the Divine Entity of One Love.

Verse 92

And from establishing the Divine Entity of One Love, Humankind will complete the Physics to the Positive Conductivity of a Universal Desire to Need to Live with the Love of our Creator – as our Creator's Spiritual Existence will function through Humankind's Creation to stabilize the Circuitry that will forever sustain the illumination of our Creator's Light for Humankind's Universal Existence of an Everlasting Life living within the Realities of a Positive Existence.

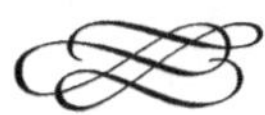

ARTICLE V
THE CROSSROADS OF HUMANKIND'S EXISTENCE

THE ILLUSTRATED DEFINITION

Verse 1

Now, by definition, the Crossroads of Humankind's Existence is the conscientious intersection of Humankind's experienced Realities of our Universal Existence within the Universe.

Verse 2

And within the Universe, there are two (2) Realities of our Universal Existence that Humankind experiences:

• The Realities of a Negative Existence – which gives meaning to the actualities of Death, and

• The Realities of a Positive Existence – which gives meaning to the actualities of Everlasting Life.And from the outset, let it be clarified that currently, Humankind is experiencing the Realities of a Negative Existence, wherein Humankind is undergoing the actualities of Death – as it is to be understood that if Humankind were experiencing the Realities of a Positive Existence, Humankind would be undergoing the actualities of Everlasting Life and would not be subjected to Death.

Verse 4

And Humankind undergoing the actualities of Death does not mean experiencing one's own demise; it is experiencing the demise of other people while being subjected to the effects of our own health and well-being diminishing – but in order to undergo the actualities of Death, one must first be given the experience of Life without the actualities of Life being Everlasting because the actualities of Life being Everlasting are the effects of never experiencing Death.

• Death, by definition, is the expiration of Life (there can be no Death without the experience of Life).

• Life, by definition, is the awareness of a created existence, and the awareness of a created existence is expirational or Everlasting depending on the operations of the Reality; and when we take a look at our Worldly living, Death dictates how we live because the operations of our Reality living upon the Earth are Negative.

Verse 5

And so, let it first be understood that "currently," Humankind is undergoing the actualities of Death while living upon the Earth because the Earth is operating within the Realities of a Negative Existence.

Verse 6

And the reason Humankind is currently undergoing the actualities of Death as the Earth is operating within the Realities of a Negative Existence is that our Creator of our Universal Existence gave Satan dominion over the Earth's living for an expirational time period of approximately 6,000 years – which means that for approximately 6,000 years, Satan has had control over the Direction of Humankind's living upon the Earth.

• Note: Having control over a Direction means having the authority to Rule or Power to Direct the management, supervision, and guidance of a particular action or operation.

Verse 7

And it is Satan's power to direct the management, supervision, and guidance of Immoral and Sinful living upon the Earth – which has influenced Humankind to generate the Negative Energies of Love that propel the Earth to operate within the Realities of a Negative Existence.

Verse 8

And while the Earth is operating within the Realities of a Negative Existence, the Direction for the Earth to operate within the Realities of a Positive Existence is at a Stop – because God has not established His Rule of Authority for the management, supervision, and guidance of Moral and Upright living upon the Earth.

• Note: Our Creator of our Universal Existence gave Satan 6,000

*years of dominion upon the Earth's living, during which time God
has No Authority over the Direction of Humankind's living upon
the Earth – which means that while Satan has had dominion over
the Earth's living, God was obligated to allow Satan to tempt and
influence Humankind in Evil and Sin.*

*• Discussion: Ask yourself, if God had Authority over the Direction
of Humankind's living upon the Earth, do you think that there
would be Evil prospering in this world?*

Verse 9

And so, in illustrating the Crossroads of Humankind's
Existence, there is (1) the Direction for the Earth to operate
within the Realities of a Negative Existence, which is
currently at a GO due to Satan having dominion over the
Earth's living (visualize this direction as traveling East to
West), and (2) the Direction for the Earth to operate within
the Realities of a Positive Existence, which is currently at a
STOP due to God's Rule of Authority not being established
upon the Earth's living (visualize this direction as traveling
North and South).

Verse 10

And just like at any crossing intersection where one
direction of travel is at a GO and the other direction of
travel is at a STOP, before the operations of travel at the
intersection can CHANGE – the direction of travel that is at
a GO must be given the opportunity to YIELD to the
authority of the direction that is at a STOP.

• *Example: The Red, Yellow, and Green traffic lights.*

Verse 11

And what this means in relation to the intersection of Humankind's experienced Realities of our Universal Existence within the Universe is that before the operations of living within the Realities of a Negative Existence can CHANGE in the direction for the Earth to operate within the Realities of a Positive Existence – Humankind must first be given the opportunity to Yield to God's Rule of Authority.

Verse 12

And this opportunity to Yield to God's Rule of Authority will be given at the End-time of Satan's 6,000 years of Dominion upon the Earth's living with the occurrence of the Apocalypse – at which time our Heavenly Father will reveal to the People of the Earth exactly who is the Messiah of Life.

Verse 13

And it is the occurrence of the Apocalypse that will signify the Crossroads of Humankind's Existence, as God will declare His Rule of Authority upon the Earth's living, with the Messiah of Life establishing the Direction for the Earth to begin operating within the Realities of a Positive Existence.

THE DIVINE PURPOSE TO THE REALITIES OF OUR UNIVERSAL EXISTENCE

Verse 14

Now, to understand why there are (2) two Realities that Humankind had to experience and why our Creator of our Universal Existence gave Satan 6,000 years of dominion upon the Earth's living, Humankind must first comprehend the Divine Purpose of the Realities of our Universal Existence.

And by definition, the Divine Purpose of the Realities of our Universal Existence, as ordained by our Creator, is to process the perfection of Humankind's creation through the Due Process of settling the Spiritual Conflict between Good and Evil.

Verse 15

And to comprehend the Divine Purpose of the Realities of our Universal Existence, we have to go back to the

Beginning when God first created Humankind in His image —because in creating Humankind in His image, God taught Humankind how to live Morally and Upright with Him, whereby reflecting the Righteous Conduct needed to generate the Positive Energies that propelled the Earth to operate within the Realities of a Positive Existence.

An important note to remember: to live with God within the Realities of a Positive Existence, Humankind was taught that it was Good to worship and obey God in accordance with our Creator's Universal Laws of Existence.

Verse 16

But in the beginning, when God created Humankind in His image, the process of creating Humankind was not complete because Humankind's creation was not perfected due to the fact that Humankind did not have the ability to exercise Free Will—meaning that while living with God within the Realities of a Positive Existence, Humankind in the Beginning was not given the opportunity to "willingly" choose to worship and obey God, thereby displaying their True Love for God.

Verse 17

And without having the ability to exercise Free Will, it seemed as if Humankind was being Forced to worship and obey God—and being Forced to worship and obey God are not actions that display True Love. Humankind displaying their True Love for God, and God reciprocating His True Love for Humankind, is how our Creator produces the

Sustenance needed to maintain Humankind's Everlasting Life.

Verse 18

But to display their True Love for God, Humankind must be given the opportunity to choose to either live with God or without God—because choosing to display the Desire to Need to Live with God means that Humankind chooses to "willingly" Worship and Obey God, just as choosing to display the Desire to Need to Live without God would mean that Humankind chooses to "willingly" not Worship and not obey God.

Verse 19

And being that Humankind in the Beginning "only" knew Good and how to live with God, in order to provide Humankind with the ability to exercise Free Will, our Creator had to permit Satan to induce Evil, whereby teaching Humankind what is Not Good and how to live without God.

Verse 20

And from Satan inducing Evil, the Realities of a Negative Existence were established—from which Humankind was given the opportunity to "willingly" choose to either display the Desire to Need to Live with God or display the Desire to Need to Live without God; and this ability to exercise Free Will is why there are (2) two Realities that Humankind had to experience.

Verse 21

Now, in establishing the Realities of a Negative Existence, Satan engaged in deceiving and tempting Humankind to be disobedient and commit Sin—thereby reflecting the Promiscuous Conduct needed to generate the Negative Energies that propel the Earth to operate within the Realities of a Negative Existence.

Verse 22

And in his endeavors to deceive and tempt Humankind to be disobedient and commit sin, Satan made the Claim that living in accordance with an Unconditional Law of existing would be "more pleasurable" than living in accordance with our Creator's Universal Laws of Existing—(basically, Satan claimed that it is more pleasurable, fun, and easier to be Evil than Good) because:

An Unconditional Law of existing is living with no requirement or obligation needed to fulfill the performance, completion, or existence of what is committed or established in the name of love and righteousness or that which is morally right.

Our Creator's Universal Laws of Existence are the established Principles that maintain the proper code of conduct in which to sustain the Righteous Qualities and Moral Behavior that capacitate the Virtues that allow our Creator's Spiritual Existence to remain in constant activation within the embodiment of Humankind's creation.

Verse 23

And with this Claim, Satan accused God of lying to Humankind—wherefrom Satan deceived a woman within the Paradise Garden of Heaven into violating our Creator's Sacred Rites of Marriage.

And by definition, our Creator's Sacred Rites of Marriage are our Creator's prescribed ceremonial order and customary form for worshipping God in accordance with our Creator's Universal Laws of Existence.

Verse 24

And it was Satan's allegation that Humankind would Not Surely Die from the Fruits of violating our Creator's Sacred Rites of Marriage that initiated the Spiritual Conflict between Good and Evil.

And by definition, the Spiritual Conflict between Good and Evil is the Power clash of a Universal Will to establish the understandings that distinguish a Positive Existence from a Negative Existence.

Verse 25

And upon the Spiritual Conflict between Good and Evil being initiated, our Creator's Omnipotent Court of Universal Law enacted a Motion that cast Satan out of Heaven and remanded him onto the Kingdoms of the Earth —which gave Satan dominion upon the Earth's living for an expiration period of approximately 6,000 years, thereby instituting the undertaking course that would produce the Trial Evidence needed to prove Satan's Claim that living in accordance with an Unconditional Law of existing is "more pleasurable" than living in accordance with our Creator's Universal Laws of Existing.

Note: Satan was not cast into Hell; he was cast out of Heaven and remanded onto the Earth—to thereby prove his Claim.

Verse 26

And with the Motion to Remand Satan onto the Kingdoms of the Earth, our Creator's Omnipotent Court of Universal Law issued a Universal Decree that closed the Gates of Heaven and ordered everyone who resided within the Kingdom of Heaven (including the person of God) and everyone who resides within the Kingdoms of the Earth to experience the Realities of a Negative Existence, whereby undertaking the Due Process of settling the Spiritual Conflict between Good and Evil.

Verse 27

Because from the closing of the Gates of Heaven, the Earth ceased operating within the Realities of a Positive Existence and began operating within the Realities of a Negative Existence—thereby giving Satan the opportunity to prove his Claim that living in accordance with an Unconditional Law of existing is "more pleasurable" than living in accordance with our Creator's Universal Laws of Existence; and this Due Process of settling the Spiritual Conflict between Good and Evil is why our Creator gave Satan 6,000 years of dominion upon the Earth's living.

IN THE OCCURRENCE OF THE APOCALYPSE

Verse 28

Now, in relation to the Due Process of settling the Spiritual Conflict between Good and Evil – it was ordained by our Creator's Omnipotent Court of Universal Law that at the End-time of Satan's 6,000 years of dominion upon the Earth's living, our Creator will initiate the occurrence of the Apocalypse.

And by definition, the Apocalypse is the Universal Phenomenon of the Manifestation of our Heavenly Father divinely revealing to the People of the Earth exactly who is the Messiah of Life.

Verse 29

And let it be clarified that the sole purpose of the Apocalypse is to identify and reveal the Messiah of Life to the People of the Earth through a Universal Phenomenon that will alleviate all confusion and leave everyone with no doubt about who actually is the Messiah of Life. Because just as there is a Messiah of Life, whose duty is to lead Humankind in the Universal Resurrection to a Positive Existence, there is a Messiah of Death, whose duty is to lure Humankind into an Eternal Existence of Death.

Verse 30

And so it is to be understood that upon the occurrence of the Apocalypse, the Universal Phenomenon thereof will be the Birth Pangs of God's Arrival – in which instances:

1. All Male Adults, except for the Messiah of Life, will begin experiencing a gradual increase in Pain within their genital organs, and

2. All Female Adults, except for the Women anointed to be our Heavenly Father's Crowned Queens of Heaven, will begin experiencing a constant Ringing within their ears, and

3. Humans not regarded as Adults, Humans deemed physically or mentally disabled, and all Animals classified as not Human will begin transitioning into a Deep Sleep for safekeeping.

Verse 31

Now, the Pain experienced by Mankind will initially serve as a "Warning" for all Male Adults to cease doing any and all activities because, as the pain increases to its extreme, the Male Adult will not be able to Stand.

Verse 32

And upon increasing to its extreme, the pain experienced by each Male Adult will not begin to subside until that Man is bowed face down on the ground in reverence to the Presence and Authority of our Heavenly Father.

Note: Address our Heavenly Father as our Heavenly Father – do not say names.

Verse 33

And as the pain subsides upon bowing face down on the ground in reverence to the Presence and Authority of our Heavenly Father, each Man will then transcend into a Spiritual Communion with our Heavenly Father, wherein that man will be given:

1. An Insight into the Realities of living within our Creator's Universal Existence of One Love,

2. An Account of the misdeeds and transgressions that he made while living upon the Earth, and

3. An Assessment of the Evil that exists within the nature of his creation.

Verse 34

Now, while Mankind is in this Spiritual Communion with our Heavenly Father, the Messiah of Life will stand to Claim his Right to sit upon our Creator's Throne – whereso to allow Womankind to confirm exactly who our Heavenly Father is divinely revealing as the Messiah of Life. Because the ringing experienced by Womankind will serve as a Calling for Womankind to locate who our Heavenly Father is divinely revealing as the Messiah of Life, in whom he will be the only Male Adult Able to stand.

Note: The Women anointed to be our Heavenly Father's Crowned Queens of Heaven, in representing Womankind, will be Gifted and in charge of publicizing and notarizing the actual identity of who our Heavenly Father is divinely revealing as the Messiah of Life.

Verse 35

But the ringing experienced by each Female Adult will not desist until that Woman acknowledges the Name of the One whom our Heavenly Father is divinely revealing as the Messiah of Life, after verifying that, to the best of her knowledge, there is No other Man able to stand as the Messiah of Life – and attempts to deviate from answering this "Calling" will result in the ringing within her ears becoming Afflictive.

Verse 36

And to acknowledge the Name of the One whom our Heavenly Father is divinely revealing as the Messiah of Life, that woman must bow face down on the ground in reverence to the Presence and Authority of our Heavenly Father and verbally proclaim the Name of the One whom our Heavenly Father is divinely revealing as the Messiah of Life.

Verse 37

And as the ringing within her ears desists upon

acknowledging the Name of the One whom our Heavenly Father is divinely revealing as the Messiah of Life, that Woman will then transcend into a Spiritual Communion with our Heavenly Father, wherein that Woman will be given:

1. An Insight into the Realities of living within our Creator's Universal Existence of One Love,

2. An Account of the misdeeds and transgressions that she made while living upon the Earth, and

3. An Assessment of the Evil that exists within the nature of her creation.

Verse 38

And after transcending into a Spiritual Communion with our Heavenly Father, all Humankind (including the Humans transitioned into a Deep Sleep) will then become seated in Audience for the Court Hearing of the Judicial proceedings for the Confrontation of Truth.

And by definition, the Judicial proceedings for the Confrontation of Truth is our Creator's Omnipotent Court of Universal Law adjudicating the process of vindicating the Messiah of Life as our Heavenly Father's Crowned King of Heaven.

Verse 39

And it is the Court Hearing of the Judicial proceedings for the Confrontation of Truth that will allow the Messiah of Life to present Humankind with the Substantiated Evidence that proves he is the Only One Worthy of sitting upon our Creator's Throne as our Heavenly Father's Crowned King of Heaven, from which Humankind must choose to either adhere to -or- oppose the Direction of the One divinely revealed by our Heavenly Father as the Messiah of Life.

Verse 40

And so, in clarity, the occurrence of the Apocalypse will signify the Crossroads of Humankind's Existence, at which time Humankind must Yield to God's Rule of Authority as the Judicial proceedings for the Confrontation of Truth begin – wherein the Messiah of Life will establish the Direction for the Earth to begin operating within the Realities of a Positive Existence, from which Humankind will be given the ability to exercise Free Will with the opportunity to "willingly" choose to either:

• display the Desire to Need to Live with the Messiah of Life as our Heavenly Father's Crowned King of Heaven, or

• display the Desire to Need to Live without the Messiah of Life as our Heavenly Father's Crowned King of Heaven.

HUMANKIND'S UNIVERSAL RESURRECTION TO A POSITIVE EXISTENCE

Verse 41

Now, from the Judicial proceedings for the Confrontation of Truth, our Creator's Omnipotent Court of Universal Law will establish God's Rule of Authority for the management, supervision, and guidance of Moral and Upright living upon the Earth, beginning with the opening of the Gates of Heaven – at which time the Messiah of Life will ascend onto our Creator's Throne as our Heavenly Father's Crowned King of Heaven, to thereby commence the Universal Trial proceedings for the Judgment of True Love.

And by definition, the Universal Trial proceedings for the Judgment of True Love is our Creator's Omnipotent Court of Universal Law's judicial process of evaluating Humankind's Desire to Need to Live "with" the Messiah of Life as our Heavenly Father's Crowned King of Heaven.

Verse 42

And in correlation with the Universal Trial proceedings for the Judgment of True Love, upon the opening of the Gates of Heaven – all those people who chose to adhere to the Direction of the One divinely revealed by our Heavenly Father as the Messiah of Life will proceed forward in Humankind's Universal Resurrection to a Positive Existence.

And by definition, Humankind's Universal Resurrection to a Positive Existence is the engagement of Humankind in the Changing of the Earth operating within the Realities of a Negative Existence, in which Humankind, in Cooperative Servitude with God's Rule of Authority, will undertake the course of action needed to overcome the Evil that exists within the nature of their creation – thereby producing and developing the habitual tendencies that generate the Energies of a Positive Existence.

Note: God's Rule of Authority is God's Government, known as our Creator's Heavenly Body, in whom are the people Anointed and Ordained by our Heavenly Father to occupy the Staff and Personnel that will maintain the operations of Universal Peace.

Verse 43

And in Humankind's Universal Resurrection to a Positive Existence, God's Rule of Authority for the management, supervision, and guidance of Moral and Upright living upon the Earth will set the Provisions and Proportions for Humankind to undertake the course of action needed to overcome the Evil that exists within the nature of their creation – and this will "fulfill" the Divine Purpose of the Realities of our Universal Existence.

Recall: the Divine Purpose of the Realities of our Universal Existence, as ordained by our Creator, is to process the Perfection of Humankind's creation through the Due Process of settling the Spiritual Conflict between Good and Evil.

Verse 44

And to fulfill the Divine Purpose of the Realities of our Universal Existence, in completing the process that perfects Humankind's creation – each and every Person must establish their own Disposition in settling the Spiritual Conflict between Good and Evil, to thereby become created "after" the Likeness of God -or- the Likeness of Satan.

Verse 45

And to establish one's own Disposition in settling the Spiritual Conflict between Good and Evil, each person must, by Free Will, either:

1. undertake the Legal Stance to produce and develop the habitual tendencies that will Stand With the Spiritual Forces of Good in subduing the Energies of a Negative Existence – from which a person will become created "after" the Likeness of God,

-or-

2. undertake the Legal Stance to induce and maintain the habitual tendencies that will Stand With the Forces of Evil in resistance to

the Energies that will sustain a Positive Existence – from which a person will become created "after" the Likeness of Satan.

Verse 46

And for the Due Process of settling the Spiritual Conflict between Good and Evil, it is the occurrence of the Apocalypse and the Judicial proceedings for the Confrontation of Truth that will establish the understandings between the Likeness of God and the Likeness of Satan – from which to allow Humankind to distinguish the Realities of a Positive Existence from the Realities of a Negative Existence; because, by definition:

(1) *The Likeness of God* is the appreciation of a Virtuous Livelihood, and it is the Lifestyle of what is Good – which establishes the understanding of a Positive Existence.

(2) *The Likeness of Satan* is the celebration of a Sinful Livelihood, and it is the Lifestyle of what is Not Good – which establishes the understanding of a Negative Existence.

Verse 47

And in order for a person to engage in the Changing of the Earth operating within the Realities of a Negative Existence, a person must, by Free Will, choose to become created "after" the Likeness of God – which means that upon the opening of the Gates of Heaven, a person must display their appreciation of a Virtuous Livelihood with God.

Note: Humankind displaying their appreciation of a Virtuous Livelihood with God basically means that upon recognizing the

*Values of God's Goodness, a person must show and prove to be
Worthy of living in accord with the Virtues of a Heavenly Lifestyle.*

Verse 48

And by Humankind undertaking the course of action needed
to overcome the Evil that exists within the nature of their
creation in accord with the Provisions and Proportions set
by God's Rule of Authority, Humankind will be Amending
and making Amends for the Wrongs that they have
committed while living upon the Earth – from which
Humankind will be undertaking the Legal Stance to produce
and develop the habitual tendencies that will Stand With the
Spiritual Forces of Good in subduing the Energies of a
Negative Existence, thereby displaying their appreciation of
a Virtuous Livelihood with God.

Verse 49

And it is Humankind Amending and making Amends for
their Wrongs in accord with the Provisions and Proportions
set by God's Rule of Authority that will not only enable God
to create Humankind "after" his Likeness, but will also
reflect the Righteous Conduct needed to generate the
Energies that will propel the Earth to continuously operate
within the Realities of a Positive Existence – thereby
displaying the Image of God; and this completes the process
that perfects Humankind's creation.

Verse 50

But let it be clarified that in perfecting Humankind's creation, being Perfect does not mean never making Mistakes or never being or doing Wrong – being Perfect means being capable of overcoming one's Imperfections by being able to Amend and/or make Amends for one's Wrongs, because:

(1) *To Amend* is to correct, improve, and/or make better.

(2) *Making Amends* is doing or giving something to make up for a loss or injury that one has caused.

Note: "Intentionally" being or doing Wrong is Evil and Sinful, but Unintentional Mistakes and Unintentional Wrongs are what we learn from to understand how to get it Right – and that is the process of Perfection.

Verse 51

And in conclusion, let it be understood that our experienced Realities within the Universe are actually the processing Phases that were designed by our Creator to perfect Humankind's creation – into which:

(1) The First processing Phase is God creating Humankind in his Image – wherein Humankind in the Beginning experienced the Realities of a Positive Existence.

(2) The Second processing Phase is our Creator giving Humankind the ability to exercise Free Will through the Due Process of settling the Spiritual Conflict between Good and Evil – wherein

Humankind is currently experiencing the Realities of a Negative Existence.

(3) The Third and Final processing Phase is God creating Humankind "after" his Likeness – wherein, in accord with the Provisions and Proportions set by God's Rule of Authority, Humankind will begin Amending and making Amends for the Wrongs they have committed while living within the Realities of a Negative Existence, thereby processing their Resurrection to the Realities of a Positive Existence; thus completing the process that perfects Humankind's creation.

Verse 52

And as we process the completion of perfecting Humankind's creation, it will be the Proceeding Measures for Humankind's Universal Resurrection to a Positive Existence that will direct, instruct, and engage Humankind in the course of action to be taken in the Changing of the Earth operating within the Realities of a Negative Existence.

www.ingramcontent.com/pod-product-compliance
Lightning Source LLC
Chambersburg PA
CBHW070851160726
48004CB00003B/1021